T0164230

The Downfall of China or CCP 3.0?

Niklas Hageback

The Downfall of China or CCP 3.0?

GAUDIUM

Gaudium Publishing
Las Vegas ◊ Oxford ◊ Palm Beach

Published in the United States of America by
Histria Books, a division of Histria LLC
7181 N. Hualapai Way
Las Vegas, NV 89166 USA
HistriaBooks.com

Gaudium Publishing is an imprint of Histria Books. Titles published under the imprints of Histria Books are exclusively distributed worldwide through the Casemate Group.

All rights reserved. No part of this book may be reprinted or reproduced or utilized in any form or by any electronic, mechanical or other means, now known or hereafter invented, including photocopying and recording, or in any information storage or retrieval system, without the permission in writing from the Publisher.

Library of Congress Control Number: 2020940077

ISBN 978-1-59211-060-5 (hardcover)
ISBN 978-1-59211-124-4 (softbound)

Copyright © 2021 by Histria Books

Table of Contents

This book is dedicated to the brave
and freedom-loving people of Hong Kong

Introduction

"Tyrants are seldom free; the cares and the instruments of their tyranny enslave them."

— George Santayana, philosopher and poet (1863-1952)

The Downfall of China or CCP 3.0 is a book for everyone that aspires to understand the enigmatic Middle Kingdom which has become so mighty that its domestic affairs are destined to play out globally as well. We have now arrived at a critical junction where the path chosen by the Chinese Communist Party (CCP) will decide whether it will face an impending downfall, or yet again can manage to radically transform itself and weather the storm.

China has faced similar transformative moments before. The CCP cleverly managed to re-invent itself from its former hardcore Marxist dogmatism, that produced nothing but misery and impoverishment, commencing with the downfall of communism in Eastern Europe in 1989. This CCP 2.0 was labelled "Socialism with Chinese characteristics," where a carefully staged semi-market capitalism was introduced. It saved the CCP from the same demise as its Eastern European peers.

The revamp of the economy has been a magnificent success, upgrading China from a Third World country to the world's second largest economy. Scale is one thing, but China's GDP per capita is still only about 25 percent of the OECD average. But now the proverbial low hanging fruit of economic development have all been picked. China has *too* much infrastructure, *too* much commercial and residential real estate for a hastily ageing and shrinking population, and hence the state commanded semi-market economy is showing signs of stagnation and coming to standstill. The ongoing trade war with the United States has exacerbated the problem. This is not surprising, as China has seen unprecedented growth for over 30 years, without any noted and extended recessions, but at the expense of an economy now leveraged to the hilt, with debt levels standing at three times its GDP.

The 'somewhat' maturing economy, the splendidly upgraded human capital, and increased interaction with the rest of the world have, however, despite the predictions of Western experts, not made China a more politically pluralistic and open society. On the contrary, China has, in fact, over the last few years become more authoritative and control-focused under the leadership of Xi Jinping who has been declared de facto leader for life. So far, there has been a kind of implicit trade-off between the CCP and its denizens; by providing them with economic prosperity and ensuring their offspring access to universities and enticing careers, its absolute political power has remained largely unquestioned. A bargain that, up until a few years ago, has been regarded as a win-win situation.

On the surface, the future prospect is promising, with a population known for not shying away from hard frugal work and having among the highest average IQs in the world. But to further progress into a fully-fledged knowledge-based economy, such as in the West or in neighboring Japan and South Korea, a decisively different tack is required. This can only come about through political reform. Thus, increased authoritarianism is creating a conundrum that will be decisive for China's future. And the party might be steering towards a head-to-head collision with the influential Chinese middle class that, either through an education in the West or travels abroad for work or holiday, have been bestowed with the insight that human rights and economic prosperity are not contradictions, but in fact complimentary necessities. The impressions formed in the outside world, with its starkly different values on the role of the state vis-à-vis the individual, has been acknowledged, and in some cases covertly adopted.

On closer inspection, problems are cropping up that are of a psychological rather than a material nature, and they now threaten the whole edifice upon which the CCP has built its power. An innovative economy can rarely be dictated to spring to action, as its main ingredient, creativity, requires critical thinking and an open mind. One cannot foresee where the manifestations of this will lead, something that by default makes any authoritarian regime with a monopoly on dogmatic truth uneasy, even paranoid.

The CCP's absolute demand for obedience and its unbending request for conformity, highlighted by its running the state and its economy in a centralized top down manner, is a particularly bad fit for an economy that requires creativity and innovation for growth. Whilst their metaphorical blood, sweat, and tears approach to achieve economic progress has been lauded, it has been stained by accusations of copycatting and undercutting competition through state sponsorship rarely available to foreign firms. Chinese claims of record numbers of patents have failed to materialize in any tangible innovations, and supposedly quantum leap research papers presenting results that are never possible to objectively test and repeat, suggest a very different story.

Accusations of state orchestrated intellectual property thefts and forced technology transfers from foreign firms operating in China are rife. This has created a seemingly unresolvable hurdle in the ongoing trade war with the United States, and indeed the rest of the world, albeit often only quietly sharing the American resentments, afraid of Chinese repercussions. If economic progress has, to a large degree, relied on stealing intellectual property and circumventing international fair-trade agreements, how much further can it extend as China's international goodwill is hastily receding amid accusations of severely violating human rights and harsh clamps downs on perceived dissidents, as well as its gross mishandling of the coronavirus outbreak? The American leadership has shrewdly identified the chink in the armor of the Chinese economy, its lack of innovation, disabled by an implicit self-imposed ban on critical thinking, which has made theft of intellectual property a key requisite for further prosperity. When and if such practices are impeded leads to the CCP's great dilemma; creativity or conformity?

The current repressive methods and demands for conformity not only risk stifling the capacity for innovation, but will also psychologically suffocate the population. The CCP is ill-equipped to handle a situation that requires guile insights into the Chinese psyche. This capacity so far apparently has been lacking from its engineering-like authoritarian leadership approach, with little acknowledgement for the truly human perspective under the false claim that China is too big for democracy and universal human rights. The CCP's heavy-handed approach now risks alienating a well-educated, well-traveled middle class, no longer easily pacified by promises of economic prosperity alone, but craving the opportunity for the self-fulfillment of goals and dreams transcending beyond merely materialism.

The future is already here, with ugly scenes of street violence playing out in Hong Kong, where Beijing's puppet regime is having to confront a radicalized middle class. This is merely a tidbit of what might unfold in mainland China itself. The situation in Hong Kong is carefully monitored by Beijing, but until now completely misunderstood by them. The CCP has become a party in dire need of soul searching, but its own grim structure prevents it from a much called for introspection.

While many speculate that a coming crisis in China will be the result of deteriorating financial conditions, burdened by an ever-increasing mountain of debt, and obviously structural factors do play a role, history, however, teaches us that societal breakdowns only occasionally coincide with economic doldrums. The trigger to such calamities is instead a collective mental stagnation prompted through a psychologically suffocating environment. This is manifested as repressive cultural norms and an authoritarian political and economic system that withholds freedom. Over time, it translates as hopelessness and (self) destruction confronting the status quo, and unless the leadership acknowledges it and embarks on reforms to alleviate the psychological distress, it will remain on the path to its downfall.

The signs of a corroding society are typically inconspicuous with the cracks in the wall appearing subtly, even insignificantly, but over time psychologically disturbing phenomena will be occur with increasing frequency. However, these are brushed under the carpet as individual irrational aberrations by the political leadership, often profoundly incompetent when it comes to psychological insights, unable to connect the dots and acknowledge a changing mental landscape. It is at this point that the seeds of its own destruction have been sown.

Chapter 1

China and the Fall of Communism

"不管黑猫白猫，捉到老鼠就是好猫"
*"It doesn't matter whether it's a black cat or a white cat,
if it catches mice, it's a good cat."*

— A quote by Deng Xiaoping in Hung Li's *China's Political
Situation and the Power Struggle in Peking* (1977), p. 107.

The fall of the Berlin Wall in 1989, and the subsequent dissolution of the U.S.S.R. a couple of years later, took the world by surprise. There exist no documented accurate forecasts of the collapse of the very foundation of an ideology and economic system that had been intensely competing with capitalism and political liberalism. It was an ideology that had enticed a surprisingly large number of admirers in the Western world, despite acknowledged insights of its darker side – mass murders, gulags, repression of human rights, and a standard of living that fell far behind what capitalism could deliver. Yet, the Che Guevara generation almost perversely found romantic appeal in Stalin, Mao Tse Tung, and other communist dictators, and idolized their aspiration of building a society void of economic and social classes, the worker's paradise. That the practical attempts of implementing such 'heavens on earth' had all but failed mattered little as fantasies superseded reality in a manner that bordered to the delusional.

When communism fell in the USSR and its Eastern European satellite states, eyes were turned to China, Cuba, North Korea, and Vietnam, among the few remaining states still adhering to the communist system, with the assumption that surely their time had also come and that they were set to follow suit. But communism was not a single animal, the hydra came in different forms and shapes, and rifts between communist states had been noted. The uneasy relationship between the USSR and China had even led to armed conflicts at the Siberian border in the early 1960s, although the lack of compatibility might be due as much to differences in the Chinese and Russian mentalities, traditionally, they never got along well, as in diverting Marxist doctrine. In 1979, the Sino-Vietnamese War led to a humiliating defeat for the Chinese by the battled-hardened and experienced Vietnamese army. In China, unlike the U.S.S.R. and its satellite states, with the possible exception of Albania and Romania, communism had taken a turn towards a bizarre cult with sectarian, almost devout religious characteristics of Mao Tse Tung.

The Cultural Revolution that had started in the early 1960s as an effort by Chairman Mao to strengthen his political power base and eliminate opposing factions in the party. It became a remarkable mixture of personal cult, where flaunting *The Little Red Book*, that contained a mixture of quotations in an array of different topics with platitudes intertwined with the occasional profound insight, was a mandatory display of loyalty. Its influence extended beyond China and it became a legendary fashion accessory among the red wine socialists in the West, whilst they rarely actually read and understood it. As the Cultural Revolution evolved, it took increasingly absurd characteristics, children were encouraged to inform authorities if their parents showed counter-revolutionary tendencies, which could come down to wearing clothes or having decorations in bourgeoisie colors or forms. This infant snitching sometimes led to fatal consequences for the parents. In addition to collapsing family structures, there was another immensely sinister outcome, the already weakened economy collapsed. In today's China, the fact that, apart from the killings of assumed class enemies, it also led to the starvation and deaths of millions is rarely spoken of and swept under the carpet. Expert estimates on the number of deaths are having to accept rounding errors in the millions. Along with this came the destruction of invaluable antique artefacts from various epochs of Chinese history as a way to start clean with a culturally and politically purified younger generation.

But the revolutionary dream was shattered. Instead, it resulted in the forced break up of families, mob rule, with a constant hunt for class enemies and scapegoats, and an economy in complete devastation. By the early 1970s, the revolutionary madness had begun to fade and a sober insight of is catastrophic consequences was dawning. China had reached an all-time low as extreme communism had exhausted itself. Slowly opening up to the world through the so-called 'ping pong diplomacy', highlighted by diplomatic recognition by the United States, and replacing Taiwan as China proper in the United Nations, was supplemented with careful studies of the capitalist system. These were the first small steps to reinvent the CCP. After Mao's demise in 1976 and the cleansing out of his cronies, the so-called Gang of Four, including his agitated widow, the residues of the Cultural Revolution could finally be buried.

With the collapse of communism in the U.S.S.R., the general view was that China would suffer a similar fate, and dissident voices, also within the CCP, started to deviate, sometimes considerably, from the existing party line, which after a twilight period culminated in the Tiananmen Square massacre in 1989, with claims that several thousand, mainly students, were killed by the armed forces and the police. In hindsight, the differing destiny of the CCP versus its peers in Europe have been declared by Sinologist researchers to be the result of a couple of factors; the CCP was far more centralized and ethnically homogenous compared to the communist party in the U.S.S.R., and could thus avoid an inner destruction of the party into various ethnic or regional factions.

For the Chinese, it meant that economic reforms could be pushed through without the risk of them being hampered by vested interests exacerbated by political infighting.[1]

The steering towards a collective leadership commenced after Mao's death in 1976, as the CCP wanted to avoid yet another disastrous personality cult, settling for consensus decisions with regard to managerial structure and changes in economic policies. This doctrine was cemented in the Third Plenum of the 11th CCP Central Committee in 1978. In a sense, this collective leadership, regulated through norms and institutions, provided a degree of democracy within the party.[2] Additional political reforms were introduced in the 1980s, such as strengthening the powers of the National People's Congress, deploying a meritocratic system for promotions, trying out some semi-democratic elections at the local level, and requiring the mandatory retirement of government officials. Even so, inherent corruption was rampant throughout the hierarchy and local fiefdoms continued to exist. There were also no attempts to establish an independent rule of law, but it was controlled and influenced by the CCP, ensuring that legal decisions would align with its policies, a condition which has remained.[3]

Whereas the CCP was centralizing political power into a committee structure through reform, it deployed a decentralized economic reform policy, in contrast to the U.S.S.R. which, in essence, had done the opposite. Regional party leaders had, to some extent, free hands to develop the provincial economies. The mandate was broadened to include fiscal policies and managing budgets, which were allowed to be distinctly crafted and implemented.[4] China introduced Special Economic Zones, the most well-known one in Shenzhen, a once sleepy and deprived fishing village with rice paddies bordering Hong Kong that now boosts its own stock market and something like an Asian version of Silicon Valley. To start with however, the focus was on lowest cost light industrial manufacturing, only gradually upgrading in the value chain, a strategy that proved highly successful.

While Deng Xiaoping further tightened political control after the massacre on Tiananmen Square, the first tastes of economic freedom triggered a thirst for more, as the riches were almost instantly in abundance. Not only was fiscal autonomy delegated to the local governments, but they were also bestowed with the capacity to establish joint ventures, property rights, allocation of land, privatization initiatives, and the formulation of rules and regulations, including their enforcement within their jurisdictions. The Russia/Soviet Union model, on the other hand, which compared to China was, from a communist perspective, a relatively industrialized country, instead focused on privatizing its heavy industries, including steel mills, automotive, and other heavy machine manufacturers, often ending up being owned by a handful of oligarchs. However, their Lada cars, and similar products, were considered a bad taste joke that were hopelessly outdated in an open market. Having to compete with Western brands, they subsequently often went out of business.[5]

China could on the other hand start with a clean slate. Ideologically, the economic reforms were a massive shift for China, promoting the accumulation of wealth, and implicitly greed, as a virtue. This was something which only a few years before had been seen as a vice that could result in long imprisonments, and even carrying the death penalty, or that during the Cultural Revolution came with the risk of being beaten to death by mob rule demanding instant street justice. For many diehard Maoists, it meant giving up, openly at least, lifelong convictions, for unlike the disillusioned citizens of the U.S.S.R. and Eastern Europe, many still believed in the righteousness of communist dogma, despite the disappointing hardships, deaths, and impoverishment that had accompanied it. However, any benchmarks and references to outside world were extremely limited as so few Chinese had an open-minded perspective to reflect on their impoverishment.

Deng Xiaoping managed, in what can only be considered logic defying and rarely hitherto endorsed by any Marxist theorists, to declare that a socialist state could adapt a market economy without actually making it capitalist.[6] To make up for what de facto was a fait accompli, in effect an unconditionally lost ideological battle, fervent Chinese nationalism was introduced to replace worn out Marxist tirades and became rampant in the propaganda efforts and the previously shunned Taoist and Confucian values were now again promoted as desired moral standards. The swift economic progress was saluted by Western observers, seen as template to be applied by stubbornly impoverished dictatorial African and Middle Eastern countries, with the view that 30 years was all it was going to take to bring any country out from an impoverished Third World status up to achieving economic prosperity that over time could near OECD's GDP per capita status. It was simply assumed, in what can only be viewed as academic ignorance, that China had followed a model that was the Holy Grail for economic development. This view chose to overlook the fact that the respect for human rights and demands for a democratic system were subdued, rather it was seen a precondition to a prosperous economy. Despite reports from Amnesty International and similar organizations on heinous crimes against humanity being committed, economists were only showing smug faces when China's lack of general human rights was brought forward.

It was assumed that with an improved economy, increased economic freedoms, including freedom to choose education, workplace, where to reside, and also the opportunity to travel abroad, eventually, the political system would also open up, becoming more pluralistic and bring with it such widespread reforms that would lead to a full-scale democracy with the right to hold divergent political opinions. But after

more than 30 years of economic progress, such hopes are now defini-
tively being quashed. It is readily apparent that a relative economic democracy is not going to be followed by political democracy in the near
future.[7]

Chapter 2

A State Commanded Economy
Only Works to a Point

"In the long run, the aggregate of decisions of individual businessmen, exercising individual judgment in a free economy, even if often mistaken, is less likely to do harm than the centralized decisions of a government, and certainly the harm is likely to be counteracted faster."

— Sir John James Cowperthwaite,
Financial Secretary, Hong Kong, 1961

Formally, the CCP introduced the paradoxical concept of a socialist market economy at the 14th National Party Congress in 1992. Reforms included pursuits to allow for and improve the efficiency of relatively free markets in order to stimulate growth. Since then, the economic growth has been continuous, albeit, over time, quite naturally, slowing down from double digit annual growth to around 6-7 percent in the last decade. Nothing in terms of output, various growth and employment statistics, although recognized as being somewhat unreliable, but also anecdotal conditions on the ground, suggest that the Chinese economy throughout this period has been dented by any protracted recessions, a truly impressive feat in itself. The economy was robust enough to withstand the Asian Financial Crisis in 1997 by implementing restrictive policies on foreign borrowing and keeping a closed capital account.[8] And the Chinese economy also endured the Global Financial Crisis in 2008, mitigating most of its negative consequences by strengthening controls to prevent capital outflows, introducing policies that restricted holding too much external debt, and simultaneously stimulated the economy by injecting credit into mainly infrastructure and real estate projects.[9] In both of these crises, the responses were remarkably apt, both in terms of content and speed, and successful in that they managed to keep the overall economy to stay on its growth course.

But what has been lauded as the Chinese economic miracle, mainly by the CCP themselves, was in fact just one of many miracles that occurred throughout North Asia. Broadly, the Chinese copied the economic growth blueprint that had been successfully implemented by countries such as Japan, South Korea and Taiwan, only that they did it some 30 years later, albeit on a larger scale. These countries operated their economic policies by a dirigisme doctrine with its growth path structured around five-year plans. The swift industrialization was initially built on cheap export goods given the low cost of labor, a model that was backed by financial support from the state to help domestic industries gain market shares on international markets, often by undercutting the prices of international competitors through state subsidies. The economic growth rates were in excess of 10 percent per annum, supported by a rapid urbanization with associated infrastructure and real estate development projects bolstering growth. With improved education levels of populations known for intellectual prowess and a capacity for not shying away from long working hours, and capital accumulation through an export driven economy, the domestic industries progressed to produce ever more sophisticated goods, eventually leaving light manufacturing behind. There was also a strong nationalist ethos in the policies to promote the countries on the world stage. However, unlike Japan and South Korea, where the state worked closely with family-run conglomerates, *keiretsu* and *chaebols* respectively, in China, state-owned enterprises have broadly taken their role.[10]

South Korea shared the dictatorship status with China, with the un-elected president Park Chung-Hee (1917-1979) declaring that the country was not ready for full democracy until the economic development had ran its course. Being in an uneasy truce with North Korea, which demanded a constant vigilance and a heavy U.S. supported military presence, his focus was to develop the economy, and indeed reduce the dependence on U.S. aid, as well as eliminating poverty prior to seeking to establish a parliamentary democracy. His tenure had a dramatic end, being murdered under mysterious circumstances, but South Korea eventually opened up to become what today is considered one of the most democratic countries in the world, where even a sitting president can be impeached, sentenced, and imprisoned. Japan was formally es-tablished as a constitutional monarchy and parliamentary democracy under post-WWII American oversight, but in effect it remained a one-party state for almost 40 years with the Liberal Democratic Party at its helm through democratic elections. A situation that was also shared in many democratic European countries, as typically a social-democratic party stayed in power throughout the 30 glorious years in Europe in the rebuild phase after World War II, endorsed by a largely satisfied elec-torate through delivering strong economic growth.[11]

It has been claimed that Deng Xiaoping took inspiration in the de-sign of the combination of economic and political systems from the au-thoritarian leader Lee Kuan Yew when they met in Singapore in 1978. Lee had managed to mix a market economy with a one-party system where any opposition or rebellious tendencies were brutally crushed, but whilst Singapore had its fair share of manufacturing, what made the city-state really thrive was as a private banking center that provided a low taxation and light regulation approach to manage fortunes made from various means from mainly South East Asian countries. But over the long run that was an economic model that China really could not follow, as it was far too large to build its economic fortunes through the arbitration of legal and tax regimes.[12]

A One-Child Policy Becoming a Zero-Child Policy

Also, unlike Japan, Taiwan, and South Korea, China introduced a harsh demographic control, the so called one-child policy that went hand-in-hand as a critical component in the efforts to modernize the mainly agricultural economy and stimulate growth through hastily reducing poverty levels, in part, arising from having to support too large families. The rapidly increasing population, in absolute numbers, was a concern with it growing from an estimated 540 million in 1949 to 940 million in 1976. A plan in the 1970s was officially approved to bring down the Chinese population to 700 million in a hundred years.[13]

The numbers vary on how many births this policy has eliminated, spanning from 200 to 400 million from its inception at the end of the 1970s to 2015. Birth rates in China has dropped from five births per woman in the early 1970s, to 2.6 at the start of the one-child policy, and stood at 1.6 in 2018. Thus, it is now far below the replacement rate of 2.1 children. As with many laws and regulations in China, there were caveats and exceptions around the one-child policy which were applied and enforced at the provincial level. For instance, small segments of ethnic minorities were allowed to have more than one child, and in many provinces, if the first-born was a daughter, parents were allowed to have another child. In all, it is estimated that roughly a third of China's fertile population were obligated by the one-child policy. The typical penalty for breaching the one-child policy was fines based on the family's income, and although the policy was meant to be all-encompassing, parts of it took a particular aim at completely preventing pregnancies for people with various types of mental and physical disabilities. It prescribed

sterilization of mentally retarded couples, or carriers of genetic disabilities, prior to being allowed to get married, but these regulations were
enforced irregularly, depending on province. Over time, the one-child
policy has been relaxed more and more, and since 2015 it was converted
into a two-child policy, as the initial plan was that of a one generation
adaption to bring population down to desired levels.[14]

The one-child policy, crude and cruel in its implementation, was
from the economic perspective to some extent unnecessary, although it
has been hailed by the CCP as one of the key success factors in achieving
economic prosperity. However, then as now, it was a well-known fact
that as women's educational levels start to improve and urbanization
takes off, these act as strong factors in themselves in the reduction of
family sizes, typically within a decade taking the number of children
born below replacement rate per fertile woman. In 2019, only about 14.6
million children were born in mainland China, the lowest in seven decades, a truly worrying number considering that the population was considerably lower a couple of generations back, despite the now relaxed
one-child policy. It is estimated that about one-third of all fertile
women, often giving reasons such as career hindrance and the high cost
of child rearing, will abstain from having any children at all. This leading to the number of births further falling to under 10 million over the
next few years, with China facing a drastic reduction of its population
over the next decades, estimated to shrink under a billion.

The ageing population, those over 60, already stands at almost 18
percent, and there is now a saying that the country might be getting old
before it is getting rich, a worrying demographic foreboding, exacerbated by the insight that China has not yet developed a full-fledged welfare society. The burden of looking after and caring for an increasingly
aging population is already taking its financial toll. The impact on the
whole economy must be not be underestimated. It is a source of grave

concern for Chinese economists. With drastically shrinking birth cohorts, fewer and fewer people will be entering the labor market, and at the other end of the demography, one of the fastest ageing populations in the world must be supported by a dwindling number of younger relatives at relatively low levels of income. The legacy of the enforced one-child policy has brought with it a conundrum for the state which is currently running a budget deficit, and has a bludgeoning mountain of debt. Hence, it can only provide elderly support and public health care to an extent, with the older generation have to rely on family support, which is keeping the savings rate too high to allow for sustained economic growth.

These high savings rates are constraining domestic consumption, which the government had hoped to boost, as a means to alleviate the slowing economy. So, the government is caught in a troublesome dilemma, to bring down the excessively high savings rate it needs to provide its citizens with assurances that the welfare system is being advanced to cater to the elderly generation's needs both now and in the future. However, with a budget deficit, the financial means to do so are not sufficient without further borrowing. Thus, the preference for saving instead of splashing out on consumption is likely to remain and is a tell-tale sign of its citizens' concern about the future, as they have to prepare financially, psychically, and psychologically to take care of their elderly parents and eventually their own geriatric needs. This is exacerbated by the low birth rates which are going to leave many elderly isolated with the unpleasant prospect of having to die alone. To many Chinese, it appears that the golden years might not turn out to be that golden after all.[15]

The one-child policy also had other demographic consequences, this with the traditional preference for boys over girls which made parents decide that their only allowed child had to be a boy, leading to female fetuses routinely being aborted. This has caused a skewed sex ratio, and there are now about 30 million more men than women in the mainland Chinese population. This is a noted problem, where a literal army of perpetual bachelors, often low-educated and typically residing in rural and destitute areas, are not able to find wives and form families, something which they are painfully aware of. In colloquial Chinese they are vulgarly referred to as 'bare branches'. However, the problem also exists at the other end of the socioeconomic and demographic scale, with well-educated affluent women in urban centers, willingly or unwillingly, abstaining from family formation, and in their 30s they are often considered as past their prime from a fertile and marital perspective, and malignly being lampooned as 'leftover women'. Albeit, in some cases, it is a self-chosen fate, through a deep-seated reluctance to marry below socio-economic class, or not being willing to accept the traditionally submissive roles of wives towards their husbands, and notably towards their stepmothers, who are often described in witch like caricature terms. This gender imbalance, and to some extent socio-economic class discrepancy, are worsening the demographic problem of low birth rates.[16]

The economic upgrade has also brought with it a difference in attitudes between the younger millennial generation and the elderly generations that lived through the calamities of the Cultural Revolution, a possibly unbridgeable perception split that will come to determine the fate of the CCP. Whilst the party propaganda still resonates with the elderly generations, accustomed to taking state-controlled news and opinions at face value without much questioning, the up till now prosperous and rapidly growing younger middle class has apparently remained lukewarm, showing little enthusiasm for the buzz words and slogans being touted. With many of the middle class now equipped with an international perspective, often having received higher education in the West, and many also worked and vacationed abroad, the party's conformist and dogmatic worldview, with few nuances, appears antagonistic and stands in contrast to the actual conditions on the ground.

They are finding the state propaganda calling for unbending and uncompromising love for China and the party appearing as simpleton platitudes, this very black and white discourse, constantly hinting at on-going foreign conspiracies but always vague on details, being interwoven with direct untruths is coming across as arrogant and overbearing. They are able to make a distinction between China and Chinese culture versus the CCP, which throughout its history often been directly hostile against Chinese traditions and culture, proactively seeking to undermine Confucian values. Such propaganda by default will fail to convey and convince any human mind, regardless of nationality, that has been educated and ingrained in critical thinking. On the contrary, it will more likely result in an alienated and rebellious attitude. The young generation are also digital natives, unlike the elderly contemporaries, knowing how to find and evaluate information for themselves, and being able to circumvent the Great Firewall and other tools of censorship. At some level, if only subconsciously, they are developing a resistance and obstinance to what is recognized as force-fed indoctrination which never is allowed to be questioned. But to confront the faltering logic and simplistic erroneous ideological tenets has so far been a taboo, and openly challenging it comes with the risk of harsh punishments, and a for certain a ruined career. As a result, open acts of dissidence have appeared only few and far between, with many choosing to accept the severe constraint of political freedoms and human rights in exchange for a what has, up till recently, been a dramatically improved economic situation, spanning over the last few decades, for most segments of the population.

A return to traditional paternalistic Confucian values, now endorsed by the CCP, which they hoped would foster patriotic sentiment, family values, and a loyalty towards the government, the word 'stability' being excessively deployed, has also broadly failed to materialize, with birth rates and family formations at record low. This as a consequence of the party in the first place successfully crushing and loathing this moral philosophy through decades of intense propaganda campaigns. Their lack of popularity being a remaining residual from the days of the Cultural Revolution.

So, despite a strong economic performance up till recently, the CCP has failed to drum up any fervent enthusiasm from the middle class, the main recipients of the economic windfall. In fact, their cool, even indifferent, attitude to patriotic symbols, such as the flag and national anthem, have not gone unnoticed by party officials, and it has led the regime to impose penalties for those who in anyway disrespect or ridicule them, a draconian penal code that has also been introduced in Hong Kong. In terms of propaganda efforts, the CCP has, by and large, failed to instigate a gratitude towards the party amongst this affluent and young middle class that will be forming the future of China.

From an Economic Point of View, Where Is China Now?

China is still far from achieving the same GDP per capita as its neighboring countries. At 2018, according to the International Monetary Fund (IMF), the Chinese GDP per capita stood just below 10,000 USD, whereas Taiwan had a GDP per capita of 53,000 USD, Japan 44,000 USD, and South Korea 41,000 USD.[17]

It took a bit more than three decades for Japan, Taiwan, and South Korea until their growth started to level out, timewise roughly where China is now along the economic development trajectory. China's neighboring countries could from that point on only advance their economy as they managed to improve productivity through upgrading to a knowledge-based economy. They were also, at the time, not in a perilous situation in terms of having a simultaneously shrinking and ageing population, as well as the high levels of debt, such as China is currently facing. The competition for well-educated employees, preferably young, kept the focus on innovative solutions and automation efforts for domestic firms, and further helped to raise productivity. The liberalization of the labor market went hand-in-hand with the overall political democratization efforts in both South Korea and Taiwan, as to allow for a societal atmosphere that promoted free creative thinking and individualism. Herein lays a wisdom that a certain element of chaos and certain levels of unknowns must be allowed to exist for a maturing economy to continue to blossom, so the cutting-edge manufacturing and high-end service sectors can develop and progress, with the view of aspiring to take an industrial lead worldwide.

There are simply too many unknown factors to centrally assess, project, and mitigate for through detailed planning which worked fine when all it came down to was copying the manufacturing processes of already existing goods, making profits through simply being cheaper and not necessarily better. It is a lesson that the CCP yet has to appreciate. Once beyond the stage of industrialization, the greater the constraints on political freedoms and civic liberties, the lower the economic output. There is a bitter pill to swallow in these insights for the Chinese government, that an open society is a necessity to progress to a knowledge-based economy, this as restrictions on knowledge and what to do with it hamper growth and innovation. But after the global financial crisis in 2008, economic reforms have come to a halt and state involvement has become more profound. The government has put more reliance on additional infrastructure and property development projects, financed mostly through domestic debt, to sustain growth and employment levels, paired with hopes on increased homegrown consumption to make up for lost export revenues. However, China is now, by and large, done in terms of infrastructure and real estate, and the problem is that these investments no longer generate the return required, and sometimes none at all, with bridges leading nowhere and apartments only built and bought for leverage-fueled speculation. The controls have also tightened for the state-owned enterprises, where the CCP, through embedded representatives, must be informed and consulted by the board of directors before any major business decisions can be made, including the setting of salaries.

It is of significance that these the state-owned enterprises, excessively bureaucratically run and inefficient in that they rarely manage to generate reasonable rates of return, still dominate vital industries including telecommunication, media, finance, key commodities, energy, and transportation. With the economy slowing down, China is trying to export its infrastructure expertise, some of which is now of world class standard, such as through the Belt and Road initiative and extensive investments in Africa, by granting loans to Third World countries to develop their infrastructure. These are, however, conditioned by demands to use Chinese workforce, equipment, and materials for the projects, in order to keep its construction industry busy and its workers employed, leading to indebting the recipient countries that are, in many cases, unable to ever pay it back. But this is an economic model that now has heavily debt-burdened China itself, as it currently has a total debt that stands at 300 percent of the GDP, including a shadow banking system whose size, by its very nature, is difficult to accurately gauge.[18]

Based on the economic development path of its neighboring countries, the path of China's economic growth, according to a reference timeline, is now set to slow down, perhaps even enter a prolonged recession. The situation might even turn out to be worse vis-à-vis what its Northern Asian peers experienced, this as China is facing some factors that all hold the propensity to advance a recession into a depression.

China is, as noted, more debt ridden than they were at the same economic stage, and are now, together with the rest of the world, facing what is likely to be a dramatic structural digital transformation change with artificial intelligence, automation, and robots replacing, more and more, manual labor in the manufacturing industry. This is also starting to negatively impact hiring in the service industry, including high-level sectors such as accountancy, law, and finance. In all, making it more difficult to find employment, also now affecting highly-educated segments of the workforce. At the aggregate level, the return on capital has been declining, as has the productivity that has been at stagnating levels for an extended period of time.[19] Economists deploying debt models, although being able to with any precision forecast the Minsky Moment is riddled with substantial inaccuracies, do predict a period of stagnation, or even recession, being a distinct possibility for the Chinese economy, as all structural factors required to trigger a downturn are now in place.[20]

China stands at the risk of getting caught in the so-called Middle Income Trap, where recently industrialized countries, through the development of its infrastructure, urbanization, and manufacturing, see its economic development stall when all the proverbial low hanging fruit have been picked, and the economy is reaching a point of exhaustion. The alleged trap consists of it becoming hard to compete in the international markets on low wages alone, as such a country has progressed above what can count as low wages, causing the previous comparative advantages over time to vaporize. And unless it can improve its productivity, this to financially motivate the higher salaries, it is thus stuck in a trap, with the economy starting to slow down. To successfully manage this upgrade requires introducing and implementing a raft of measures, something which previously Japan, South Korea, and Taiwan completed, and they are actually one of the few examples that managed to overcome this Middle Income Trap, efforts which were characterized by heavy investments into higher education, research and development, but also allowing for economic and political liberalization. Thus, the transition up the productivity ladder to be able to produce more value adding high-end advanced products and services, necessitates the retraining of workers, in particular an emphasis on engineering and computer science skills, and a focus on innovation that must be in the forefront. To simply copy, illegally or not, existing products, and undercutting competition through price alone, will not tilt an economy out of the Middle Income Trap.

But China has instead moved towards more authoritarianism, with Xi Jinping cracking down hard on dissidents. Any opposition in the party is routinely accused of corruption, or similar non-related crimes, and imprisoned in order to centralize his power and control of the party. Xi has effectively become de facto leader for life. But surpassing the Middle Income Trap requires the insight that creativity cannot be ordered to spring into action. The way forward instead requires democratic political reforms and market liberalization. As David Dollar points out:

> Authoritarian countries evidence very sharply diminishing marginal returns, suggesting that these countries can start an accumulation-driven growth process that takes them from low to middle income, but that they lack the innovation capacity to continue growth from middle to high income.[21]

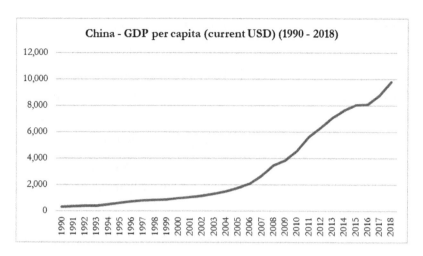

Figure 1) China, GDP per capita (current USD), 1990 - 2018. Source: The World Bank, World Development Indicators. https://data.worldbank.org/indicator/NY.GDP.PCAP.CD?locations=CN

Figure 2) China - Gross Domestic Savings (% of GDP) 1990 - 2017. Source: The World Bank, World Development Indicators. https://data.worldbank.org/indicator/

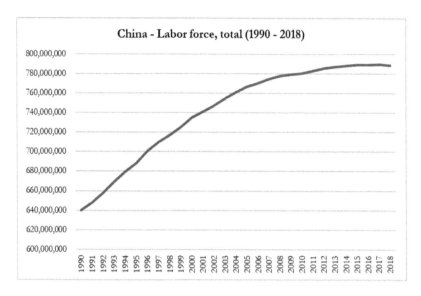

Figure 3) China - Labor Force, total 1990 - 2018. Source: The World Bank, World Development Indicators.
https://data.worldbank.org/indicator/

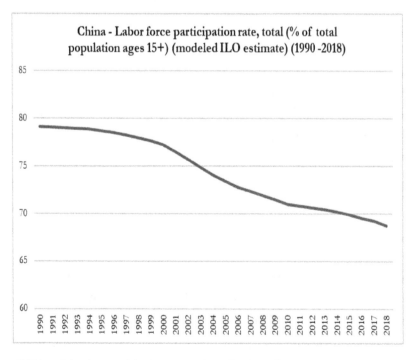

Figure 4) China - Labor force participation rate, total (% of total population ages 15+) (modeled ILO esti-
mate). 1990 - 2018. Source: The World Bank, World Development Indicators.
https://data.worldbank.org/indicator/

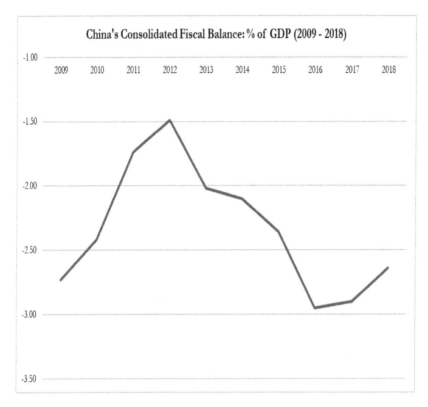

Figure 5) China's Consolidated Fiscal Balance: % of GDP. 2009 - 2018. Source: CEIC Data.
https://www.ceicdata.com/en/indicator/china/consolidated-fiscal-balance--of-nominal-gdp

As figure 1) highlights, China is now reaching about 10,000 USD GDP per capita, a level where the Middle Income Trap typically closes, and progressing onwards has proven a difficult undertaking. Reasons for this have often been demographics, as the surplus of labor dwindles due to a falling natural population growth and the countries start to age before they have gotten rich, with both the state and households having to spend disproportional resources on elderly care, drawing investment away from income generating sectors. But also, to move above and beyond the Middle Income Trap requires that domestic companies are capable of innovating and taking the lead in various industries, which requires a completely different mindset than simply copying existing goods and services. Such conditions might be worsened through institutions and a political system that are not conducive to stimulate creativity.

Figure 2) indicates an awareness of the coming demographic consequences and uncertainty about the future that the CCP has not been able to alleviate, this as the savings rate has remained high despite the government's efforts to try to boost homegrown consumption.

Figures 3) and 4) highlight that the workforce is no longer growing but has levelled out, and will from here on be shrinking even faster as birth rates are dropping to record low levels, and also the work participation rates are at the same time falling, now standing at below 70 percent, in essence, fewer and fewer people on relatively low incomes will have to support a hastily ageing population.

Figure 5) shows that despite China has been reporting growth number at around 6-7 percent per annum, its consolidated fiscal balance has remained in negative territory over the last ten years.

If the repressive stance remains, the risk of a downward spiraling vicious circle is obvious, as the economy further loses steam, even going in reverse, with the authorities worried about ensuing social unrest, and trying to pre-empt any such situation. These extraordinary harsh measures risk in themselves to provoke citizens to engage in rebellious activities and turmoil, which then simply come to serve as evidence that the tough measures were all along justified. The risk for internal conflicts will remain as long as the economy is faltering and the relative civic freedoms are further curtailed and even withdrawn.

Thus, authoritarianism works both ways in economic development, at the first stage, when attempting to industrialize, having the whole nation and its institutions moving in the same direction, by being politically able to coordinate all efforts and resources toward a few goals will in all likelihood provide a distinct advantage. This rather than having to go through a democratic process with vested interests that can block decisions that might be beneficial overall for the whole economy, which do happen frequently, such as rejecting a decision to build (nuclear) power plants, even as that at the aggregate level can lower energy costs and reduce the dependence on energy imports. For China, it was coined as the *Beijing Consensus Model*, where a party committee was finding common ground amongst its members to move the economy forward. But once the industrialization phase has run its course, continuing to operate on a state-commanded, central planning style economic doctrine will struggle to deliver. What is instead required is a society that is more tolerant to perceived deviations from constraining norms, both cultural, economic, and political. Also, the legal system needs transparency and judicial independence, where the outcome of a legal case, despite the merits in any directions, no longer by default goes in the favor of the claimant with the best political contacts.[22]

What is Next for China?

China is now at a critical junction when it comes to its growth trajectory, as the economy is slowing down, the factors behind these are plenty fold; an ongoing trade war where China is being accused of predatory trade practices by gaming international trade rules through parasitic tactics, and with the U.S. retaliating with damaging trade tariffs that now are severely hurting its export industries. But also, a rapidly ageing population with the lowest birth rates in generations, that over the coming decades will lead to a significantly smaller population than its current roughly 1.4 billion citizens. The slowing and maturing economy where the old trick of pouring money into infrastructure and real estate, and through cheap labor and state subsidies undercutting competition on the world market, no longer seems to pay off. It appears that the risk of China getting stuck in the Middle Income Trap is becoming a reality that will require the introduction of a new doctrine more geared towards the knowledge-based economy.

However, with China being only at the 10,000 USD GDP per capita level, in order to move forward, the government has proactively embarking on a lending spree, this time to try and boost domestic consumption, but that is adding to an already worryingly high debt rate for a country at their economic status. Albeit, it is mostly domestically generated credit, which means that the debt mountain can keep on growing for years before becoming acutely system threatening, to project indebted economies' Minsky moment has proven virtually impossible for even the most seasoned economists and central bankers to do. But what possibly stands as the biggest hindrance for upgrading China to a knowledge-based economy might be the CCP itself, with its increasing repression of its population, having introduced a social credit system that by which even the nightmarish descriptions from George Orwell's epic work about a Big Brother control state, *1984*, pales in comparison.

All historical experiences provide the insights that paring an authoritarian repressive societal system with a culture that spurs creativity and innovation, regardless of whether it aims for artistic, industrial, or scientific endeavors, has proven over the long-term to be a futile undertaking. Likely being aware of the historical precedents, the leadership of the CCP knows that the economic future, and by extension their own political survival, as articulated in its Made in China 2025 strategy, rests on developing an innovative economy. But for a society where conformity comes first, what room is there really for creative persons to roam freely?

Chapter 3

The Enemy of Creativity is Conformity

"Americans are not smarter than the Chinese. The only thing that holds China back, is that the nature of dissent and creativity are related."

— Steve Blank, Silicon Valley entrepreneur,
"Does top-down, state-led innovation work? Just ask Silicon Valley,"
SCMP, 15 June, 2019

When it comes to culture, extending to child rearing and the educational system, academia acknowledges pronounced differences between China and the West. And whilst findings from cultural studies must be considered on a sliding relative scale rather than absolutes, consistent deviations highlighted in generalized patterns, especially if manifesting across various cultural stratums, do provide insights that facilitate the understanding and help to predict both individual and collective behavior. These average behavioral patterns often become normative, with any aberrations being frowned upon, and even risk ostracizing the perceived transgressor.

So, what are these noted differences? Compared to the West, Chinese culture places more value on unity and conformity. The average Westerner versus the average mainland Chinese tend to differ in that the former actively seeks independence with individual goals, that need not necessarily to be aligned with the overarching collective ones, whereas the latter is conditioned by a culture that seeks to align the group and its objectives. In short, the West comes across as more individualist societies, whereas mainland China is collectivist society. These attitudes influence social relationships, which in the Chinese way is arranged through a more structured hierarchy. According to Confucian principles, family precedes strangers, the older generation precedes the younger generation, and men precede women, and, in particular, elderly men stand at the top of the pyramidically-shaped ranking, against which any resentment or critique best are avoided, even when merited, as that constitutes a grand social gaffe.

Through this pecking order, personal independence and preferences are, at least outwardly, expected to be sacrificed. The Western mindset does not make this distinct delineation between family and friends, men and women, and elderly people are, on the contrary, often viewed with a certain disdain as lesser-knowing, with wisdom being a vocabulary that long has become absent in Western society. The formation of social relationship along these more ancient standards was, by and large, phased out from Western culture over the last two generations, instead putting the uniqueness of the individual, albeit not always stringently practiced, in the forefront.

These cultural traits also make their marks in child-rearing and the educational system. Buzz words such as *Tiger Moms* and *China's examination hell* have come to epitomize the Chinese educational system, traits that are also shared in other North Asian countries. It is a system where the focus of the studies is overwhelmingly to pass tests, and where the test scores (solely) decide whether the student can be elevated to the next educational level. Room for critical analysis, and challenging, or even confronting, teachers and the curriculum are simply out of the question, with any signs of rebellion being met with a heavy-handed approach that in the Western educational system would only be labelled as child abuse. And this authoritarian ethos extends up to tertiary levels, completing the educational system's molding of the young generation.

Thereafter, an entry level position in the already colossal and expanding bureaucracy, or in some of the huge state-controlled enterprises, will operate much on the same principles, where any critique, although hardly ever occurring, against managerial decisions from underlings, even when constructive in nature, are considered audacious and affrontive. It becomes a corporate culture full of yea-sayers, blindly following managerial instructions and orders, minimizing the opportunity to any creative and performance enhancing suggestions to the point of them being non-existent. Throughout the educational system, and extending into most of the work life, the emphasis is on homogenization, where methods of discipline and fear-based motivational tools are key ingredients until this way of life has become so second nature that it is self-regulating.

The focus on maintaining order and applying strict routine with a readiness to quickly clamp down on any rebellious features is mirrored in the parenting as it is what much of the parent-child relationship evolves around. The children's' cognitive abilities are thus forced into a narrow educational strand where anything outside it is shunned, because it will not deliver the desired high scores in tests. In such an educational environment, an insight which even mainland Chinese educational scholars agree on, a child's natural curiosity and capacity for diverse and independent thinking will not evolve to its full capacity. However, the dire need for a creative and innovative workforce remains, with the demand for them rapidly increasing, but the question of how it will actually be achieved is usually met with silence by accountable authorities. This as the key ingredient, critical thinking, unobstructed by a curriculum with emphasis on certain dogma and taboo areas that can never be discussed, implicitly suppress and dwarfs this mental faculty, as it can simply never be allowed to operate without boundaries. Introducing critical and creative thinking into an authoritative educational system becomes a conundrum not only from the point of view to assess such an elusive topic in a score obsessed system, but also from the political perspective, as they can never be sure where it will be going theme wise. The creative thoughts of young people can eventually also question the legitimacy of an undemocratic system that is fiercely denying civic liberties, including free speech. And the hopes that Western-educated students returning back to China, bringing in fresh perspectives on how an innovative environment operates in some areas but not in others has so far failed to materialize. This as the universities or corporations they are re-introduced to still operate on dogma rather than free research (and speech).

But so far, the ethos has relied on the hopeful wish that necessity fosters innovation, and that the infinite wisdom of the party will craft the means and ways required to achieve groundbreaking innovation. In Western exchange programs, there are many examples where academically well-groomed mainland Chinese students excel way and above their peers, especially in mathematics and natural sciences, but fail completely in so called liberal studies, such as being queried "And, what do you think?" and other open ended questions about certain ill-defined topics that lack a single interpretation and answer. Often, they go at great length to devise strategies to avoid such situations, or simply craft a plethora of pre-rehearsed platitudes to disarm the request for critical thinking, trying to make up for it through the memorization part of the learning experience.

There have been academic attempts to better understand the diverging thought processes between Asians and Westerners. In his 2003 book, *The Geography of Thought: How Asians and Westerners Think Differently and Why*, the American social psychologist Richard E. Nisbett sought to highlight the differences between Chinese (East Asian) form of thinking versus Western thinking, as it originated in the antique Greek philosophy. The delineation is between interdependence vis-à-vis independence. To his point, Chinese thought patterns harmonize, by seeking out unity and commonality in which relationships between the parts and optimization of the whole are more important than the individual parts themselves. According to Nisbett, Western-style thinking aims to breaking up the whole into its atomic units, discrete and reductionist, seeking solutions to problems by dissolving rather than unifying them to a higher level. In essence, whole versus units, or a collectivistic approach seeking out the common denominators, preferring generalizations and purging discrepancies and the sui generis, this being in glaring opposition to thought patterns that seeks individualism and cherish uniqueness. Nisbett's study becomes a palpable observation when ascertaining in which thought system that creativity and innovation has the greatest chance to flourish. This distinction is also highlighted in education, where rote learning and repetitive writing of characters, all acts of copying, have failed to entice Western pedagogy. And the attitude to copying stands at the heart of the ongoing trade war with the U.S., something considered a severe transgression in the West where academic cheating has crushed careers, even when discovered decades later.[23]

What is Creativity Really?

The renowned Spanish painter Pablo Picasso was once quoted as saying; "every act of creation is first of all an act of destruction." On the surface, Picasso's comment might completely contravene the very definition of creativity, but the act of creating something innovative is often preceded by challenging and confronting pre-conceived notions and assumptions on how to do things, and an attack on the normative thought patterns that stands as the doctrine of a particular scientific edifice. In the words of the American philosopher Thomas Kuhn (1922-1996), a creative breakthrough can signify a scientific paradigm shift. As creativity transcends all areas of human activities, not only science and the arts, but also politics, its influences can become contagious and set trends that reverberate throughout the whole of society. To this point, the creative, risk-seeking personality is sometimes connected with transgressions, as creativity can be viewed as a break with existing rules and defining new ways of doing things, not unusually completely deviating from existing methods.

Creative people are often personality wise considered eccentric and quirky, extending to being rebellious, even intimidating, and not afraid of confronting and questioning authority, both as manifested in its representatives and the perceived truths around which society gyrates. A noted psychological truth, whilst rarely recognized in an authoritarian setting, is that creativity brings with it a dynamism that is basically uncontrollable, and trying too hard to harness it risks eliminating it. Some philosophical research papers have shown a linkage between creativity and dishonesty, traits working in both directions; creativity may lead to dishonesty, and vice versa, dishonesty may lead to creativity, and creative people have in studies shown to be more likely to bend rules and even break laws.[24] Whilst this might be a peculiar observation and obviously disturbing from an ethical perspective, however the term "thinking outside the box" can and should be loosely equated as "thinking outside the existing rules."[25] Hence, creative thinking typically requires that one break some, but maybe not all, rules within a domain to allow for and construct associations between previously unconnected cognitive elements. The resulting unusual mental conjunctions then serve as the basis for exploring and elaborating on novel ideas.[26]

Research on creativity gives further evidence on what is required to prosper from an innovative perspective. This includes removing organizational hindrances introduced through standardization, and being vigilant on an often overabundance of rules and bureaucracy as these prevent the many good suggestions that could improve performance.

These are often of a nonlinear and an unexpected nature, which by default rarely makes them appreciated, in particular if they come from the wrong level (read: too junior) in the hierarchy.[27]

Thus, unconducive environments for creative activities are characterized by conformity, codified through hierarchical systems with a wide array of rules and regulation stipulating behavior and where any deviances thereof are often strongly condemned. There are really no examples of authoritarian regimes under which creativity has been able to blossom over the longer term. In the U.S.S.R., during the cold war, there was little to show in terms of creative art and science, and its temporary lead in the space race was founded on captured German World War II rocket scientists and their technological insights, highlighted through the launch of the world's first satellite, *Sputnik*, in 1957, and the cosmonaut Yuri Gagarin as the first man in space in 1961. From there on, the leveraging of Nazi-derived technology faded and when left to its own device innovation amounted to little. Their nuclear weapons program was achieved through espionage, and the U.S.S.R. was quickly outmatched by NASA's efforts.

It has proven very difficult to direct creativity into specific research areas whilst at the same time restricting it for others. The nature of creativity does not work that way, as creative individuals with rebellious personalities will sooner or later find themselves in trouble in a dictatorial society, and often, through deliberate provocations, coming up with ideas that challenge what are considered unquestionable truths. This as conformist societies, which sometimes also can be of a democratic constitution, tend to maintain one single interpretation of reality, but creativity, independent of domain, requires going beyond such limitations and, as required, challenging the prescribed conventional wisdom. Through a repressive educational system, creative and rebellious natures are typically weeded out at an early stage, never being allowed to fully flourish and pursue their entrepreneurial and creative talents.

The prerequisite for creativity, namely a capacity for critical and prob- ing thinking and with that a disdain for absolute truths, is rarely an ap- preciated talent in a political system that has developed its edifice on dogma that cannot be challenged without the risk for persecution. And herein lies the problem, creativity must by its definition not be con- tained to certain domains. It must be allowed to be free flowing given its transcending and transgressional nature. Thus, if the mainland Chi- nese educational system embarks on efforts to foster and promote a gen- eral creative environment, it will eventually spill over to both political and artistic creativity, areas which have been declared no-go zones by the CCP.

In a research paper studying the impact of cultural individualism and collectivism on creativity among American and Chinese highly ed- ucated adults, the result suggests that cultural background influences both creative potential and the subsequent achievements. The largely individualist Americans displayed significantly higher scores on a measure of creative potential than the more collectively-inclined Chi- nese, and the researchers concluded that the difference was due to cul- turally induced traits rather than cognitive ability, this as the Chinese on average had significantly higher scores in mathematics.[28]

Hence, despite the high educational levels, from a test score point of view, it is doubtful whether Chinese universities will be able to take the lead and set global research standards. The governance of the Chi- nese state-owned universities is top-down heavy, where most principal decisions are left to party apparatchiks, always ensuring that decisions do not deviate from the party line. In such an environment, self-censor- ship is applied to not mistakenly say or suggest something that could be career limiting. Freedoms to pursue ideas in any direction is simply not part of such a governance model, as faculty members are subject to party control and need to align to its overall strategy. And party supervision of higher education has further increased under Xi Jinping's leadership, where student literature for the various curriculums, especially foreign ones, are being carefully scrutinized for any unsuitable topics or viewpoints.

Until recently, China has been able to enjoy the late comer's advantage, modelling both its higher education and various industries by copying global market leaders and standards to the point it aligns with the CCP's ambitions. Anything falling outside theses, such as liberal studies, or at least the contents thereof, are mostly being ignored or heavily re-phrased, sometimes beyond recognition. However, going from copycatting to taking a leadership role in academia and science requires a vastly different approach, with the level of innovations being stifled by the CCP's authoritarian and repressive approach in that it demands a monopoly on truth with any dissident deviation being severely punished, amongst other methods, through its social credit system which also assigns collective guilt. The rebellious and free-spirited Steve Jobs and Elon Musk characters of the world would have huge difficulties fitting in in today's China and would likely never have been able to achieve what they have done in the free-wielding American culture, as they, at some point, would have confronted the regime and various representatives of the bureaucracy with potentially damaging consequences for them.

There Are Patents and then There Are Patents...

"Lack of innovation is the 'Achilles heel' of China's economy."

— President Xi Jinping, from a speech made in January 2016 and published a year later in Qiu Shi.

In the traditional Chinese way of thinking, copying is not frowned upon but rather encouraged, where parroting a master's work is considered flattering, a perspective which is also incorporating the aloof perspective that theft of intellectual property is not to be recognized as a crime. This provides the cultural explanation to the Chinese legal system's indifference and lax attitude to infringements of intellectual property rights. Thus, demands from U.S. and other countries that a fair intellectual property law must be implemented and enforced by Chinese authorities contradicts the long standing historical cultural and judicial traditions that the respect for uniqueness is subordinate to a higher common good.

The open, but rarely talked of, secret behind the Chinese economic growth has been the leverage, in many cases illicit, of existing intellectual property. It has granted substantial benefits to Chinese firms through circumventing the high costs and risks of having to engage in research and development, and instead being supplemented by copies of blueprints and models from international peers, provided through various means, such as technology transfers and outright state sponsored industrial espionage. It left them with just having to focus on the manufacturing process, which costs often are, to some extent, state subsidized to undercut foreign competition and gain market shares. The risk of lawsuits and repercussions from international firms have, until recently, been miniscule as the fear of retaliation from China has been overwhelming. But now as China is increasingly accused of not protecting foreign intellectual property, allowing for it to be copied, and sometimes even audaciously claimed as domestically-developed Chinese technology. Foreign companies wanting to operate in China are required to transfer technology and know-how, under the pretext of safeguarding national security, to Chinese authorities. Later, they often find that these have been passed on to their Chinese competitors. And what technology they cannot access through this forced transfer, there exists plenty fold of allegations that through widespread industrial espionage, orchestrated by the various security agencies, they have looted intellectual property from industry leaders and universities in the West.

However, China claims that it has now domestically developed a technological leadership, pointing to the number of filed patents, which is one way to gauge and metricize the level of innovation. Patents are used to secure exclusive rights to an invention for a number of years, requiring the patent office to request specific details of the design or contraption to be able to assess its uniqueness and to protect it from infringements. So, by determining the trends in the number of patent applications, it can provide an insight to the number of innovations materializing thereof, and the relative value of the patent can be gauged through how many times it has been cited. The numbers of patents have quite literally exploded in China, in all sectors. Between 2008 and 2017, the number of patent applications filed in China rose from 204,000 to 1,300,000, a 600 percent increase, in comparison the U.S. only saw a 20 percent increase, from 429,000 to 525,000 in the same time period.[29]

The assumption has been that it would translate into an exponentially increasing number of domestic innovations. However, the numbers do not tally, few experts in the various industry sectors can point to specific Chinese innovations cropping up over the last decade. Hence, what is going on?

In China, there are three different categories of patents: invention, utility model and design. Invention patents are defined as new ideas that represent notable progress and is what typically is understood as being a patent proper, these represents 23 percent of all patents granted in 2017. Utility model and design are thus lower quality patent applications, and by many international experts seen as virtually worthless, as 91 percent of all design patents that had been granted in 2013, had been discarded by their innovators by 2017 as they no longer thought it worthwhile to pay the fees to the patent office. For utility models, that number was 61 percent, and for invention patents, the disposal rate was 37 percent. For the U.S., the corresponding disposal number for the same time period was only about 14 percent.

With patents coming in different forms, also differing between jurisdictions, what however is considered to be the premium standard is the triadic patent family, which are patents filed jointly to the Japan Patent Office (JPO), the United States Patent and Trademark Office (USPTO), and the European Patent Office (EPO), as a way to secure a broader protection of intellectual property which helps the inventor commercialize his innovation and reduce the risk for intellectual property theft. In 2015, the application for triadic patents were only a mere 2,889 for China, while the U.S. filed 14,886, and Japan 17,361 patents. This has put serious doubts on the quality of Chinese patents, and brought forward the suspicion that universities and companies are being encouraged, through subsidies and other incentives, by the authorities to file patents for innovations that are not really innovations, in order to proclaim China as a world-leading center of excellence when it comes to creativity. Quantity has been allowed to precede quality. The low retention rates across all sectors of patent filings highlights the systematic problem and puts China's Made in China 2025 program, which aspires to make the country a global leader in key technology sectors, including artificial intelligence, in jeopardy. With such low quality, and even absence of domestic innovations and innovators, resorting to forced technology transfer and theft of intellectual property remains the only option, but it will never allow China to lead, merely copy and follow, and unable to set standards.[30]

But if China now is increasingly leaving the manufacturing phase of economic development behind, either through outsourcing, retrieval of plants back to North America or Europe, and ongoing automation, its annual cohorts of youths entering the labor market each year will find fewer and fewer available entry positions. And if the education system by default makes them less suitable for creative work, and the pipeline to copy or steal intellectual property is becoming increasingly reduced, a structural crisis is looming which till now has been alleviated through debt accumulation and a budget deficit that has proven hard to close. The problem is being painfully admitted and recognized by the leadership, as this chapter's initial quote from Xi Jinping indicates, echoing the warning of former Premier Li Keqiang in 2015;

> China's economic growth model remains inefficient; our capacity for innovation is insufficient; overcapacity is a pronounced problem; and the foundation of agriculture is weak.[31]

Chapter 4

The Stability – Instability Paradox

"Unexpressed emotions will never die. They are buried alive and will come forth later in uglier ways."

— Sigmund Freud, Austrian psychoanalyst (1856-1939)

The psychological atmosphere in a society guided by a political doctrine that cannot be questioned means that there come to exist taboo areas, which over time suffocate the public discourse with a psychological shadow coming in existence with which the population must conform. The deviation between the discourse of 'allowed' themes versus an unbending and uncompromising reality triggers psychological denials. The excessive amount of perceptions that are forced to be excluded from such a constrained world view increases the risk of mental unhealth as it creates a distorted view of the world that eventually becomes unsustainable and difficult to adhere to without the repression mechanism working in overdrive.

In a society where the focus is on a certain set of norms that are *expected* to be shared by its citizens and enforced through various means, including an educational system where only a single viewpoint is promoted, as well as never ending propaganda campaigns throughout various media channels, this extended collective focus comes at the expense of individual development. Eventually, traits of stagnation, extending to apathy, are noticed. Individual initiatives across many aspects of life come with the risk of being perceived as a non-conformist or to be singled out as an instigator of social disharmony.

Thus, there is a lack of endurance and courage to stand-up against all the propaganda being produced, so the platitudes and simpleton buzzwords are parroted until they are a formative part of the narrative. It means there will be little in terms of thoughtful understanding of the dominating ideology, as repetitive platitudes come to suffice, and, as such, truly open debates are being avoided or outright banned as the loyalists rarely can speak up for their views which are merely slogans. So, any opposition against these dogmas can often shock the zealot supporters of the regime that the only response they can muster are a tirade of profanities or declaring their opponents mentally ill. It becomes a distinct contrast to a pluralist society that recognizes and addresses its problems through debate and allows for and encourages disparate views. But a dogmatic ideology rarely acknowledges any weaknesses in its creed and works to sustain an ideal view of itself, with problems being covered up or re-phrased, increasing the tendencies of psychological repression.

In China, any mention of the disastrous consequences of the Cultural Revolution or the Tiananmen Square massacre are prominent examples of what cannot be freely discussed but are being severely limited, with only CCP's rigid and minimalistic perspective of the distressing events being allowed. The demand for political cleanliness is enhanced by the authorities' efforts to ban words deemed as heretical, introducing euphemisms, in effect trying to outlaw illegal thoughts, something very notable in Chinese media. But with the ban of critical thinking, the human collective regresses to infantilism and hibernation as anything that confronts the prescribed worldview and appears problematic must be silenced and brushed under the carpet.

Such an oppressive environment allows for people with psychopathic traits to prosper and to come to power, as neurotic and narcissistic conditions inevitably become the reigning norm, even seen as an ideal to adhere to and a lack of self-awareness comes to qualify as a career enhancing characteristic. A political school of thought drawing heavily on insights of the psychological make-up of political leadership, particularly focused on studying the development of authoritarian regimes and how they collapsed. Its main proponent was the Polish psychiatrist Andrzej Łobaczewski (1921-2007) who proposed the term pathocracy for governments dominated by psychopathic individuals that show a lack of remorse and empathy, disinhibited and egoistical to the point of being narcissist. Łobaczewski, being of Polish origin, no doubt developed the theory with the communist regimes of Eastern Europe and the U.S.S.R. in mind. A pathocracy generally quickly evolves into a totalitarian political system.

According to Łobaczewski, this kind of political system could develop in societies that are not psychologically equipped or mature enough to deal with individuals of an abnormal psychological make-up. In such an atmosphere, psychopaths find it easier to progress on the career ladder, as normal psychological reactions, with their affiliated norms and values, have been put out of play, allowing them to thrive as their psychological dispositions align well with the abnormal settings. Psychopaths are an integral part of mankind, and Łobaczewski viewed their characteristics as innate, meaning that, for these psychopaths, rules and norms that regulate normal human behavior such as reciprocation and a sense for fairness, do not apply by default, and hence it becomes hard to adjust them. Thus, they blatantly circumvent and challenges human rights without much feeling of guilt. In such a mental setting, over time, the pathological individuals in the population start to rise through the ranks and infiltrate political parties, religious and civic organizations, eventually gaining leadership, perverting the original doctrines for their own purposes, and using them to manipulate society.

This rise to power, Łobaczewski considered part of the *ponerogenic* process. And as their power accumulates, the sense of normal in society is distorted so that the behavior of pathological groups becomes the norm and what is perceived as being common sense is regarded as skewed and unnatural. To uphold their leadership, they typically deploy censoring of the media. By taking control of the educational system, they introduce methods such as indoctrination and selection of academic leadership based on political affiliation, as well as adjusting the curriculum to include mandatory subjects that align with their dogmatic beliefs.

Over time, a political system based on loyalty rather than merit by default will regress to incompetence and corruption. Inefficient management will fritter resources and tax revenues, and, eventually, the discrepancy between the lofty political ideals versus reality becomes so obvious and so hard to gloss over with propaganda and platitudes, that eventually the regime is forced to acknowledge its own shortcomings. This is often combined with blaming scapegoats typically accused of acting in concerted conspiracies with sinister foreign forces. This leads to widespread contempt and dissatisfaction amongst the population, and if it gains momentum, the government's legitimacy becomes unsustainable. The regime is often undermined through humor manifested as mockery, sarcasm, and irony, pointing out absurdities and deficiencies in the oppressive political system and the black and white propaganda campaigns. As such, a pattern with predictable characteristics in the rise and fall of a pathocracy can be observed, and it typically coincides with economic peaks and troughs, however often interacting as incompetent governments themselves tend to cause economic difficulties.[32]

When Power is the Only Political Goal, Coercion is the Only Tool

Much of the CCP's monopoly on power rests on the silent endorsement of its newly formed middle class. They were provided with some economic freedoms and prosperity, but nothing in comparison to their more affluent neighboring countries. Their human rights, such as being able to choose ones' education, work place, and the right to travel abroad, are highly limited and conditioned, all in exchange for obedience and, superficially at least, loyalty. But this relationship is not all that straightforward. It also comes with an overhanging threat, with the reminiscence from the Tiananmen Square massacre fresh in mind, that any opposition would be quashed in blood. This tacit trade-off might now be fading, as this affluent socio-economic group is equipped with an international perspective, often through a Western education and access to international media. They are also prosperous and well-educated enough to see through any simpleton propaganda. By constantly being presented with a world in black-and-white when they are cognitively capable to experience reality as it really is, in shades of grey, these antics come across as lacking in sophistication, and they are met with a healthy skepticism, even disdain, however rarely given a public voice, considering the risks such acts carry. Commentary from the CCP on world affairs often include a thinly veiled racism, bizarrely enough directed toward its own population, where any domestic outcries against the party' policies are often blamed on gullible Chinese being duped by ominous cosmopolitan forces – usually the CIA. Somehow it is implicitly assumed that the Chinese as an ethnic group are naïve and susceptible to deception, easily being led astray from making the politically correct choices, and that without the CCP's paternalistic care, any Chinese, whether educated or not, are vulnerable and need perpetual protection, and constant vigilance must be enforced. This push to cleanse China of foreign influences has extended to forcing out international non-governmental organizations, often being accused of espionage or meddling in domestic affairs, and the Chinese media often castigates foreigners' negative influence on the Chinese mindset.

The Chinese government is constantly looking for signs of transgressions, but in a perverse sense the pre-empting of any tendencies of rebellion is what often historically trigger uprisings. Any promotional activities of democracy or human rights is by default seen as a U.S., or Western, destabilizing conspiracy, seeking to undermine CCP's monopoly of power. Hence, anything Western is viewed with a certain suspicion as being subversive, in itself an irony, as their founding ideology, *communism*, was an integral part of Western political philosophy and subversive enough in nature to overthrow the millennia old empirical society, with the forming of the CCP involving several foreigners as advisers. The quest for purity has become a key concern and Xi Jinping has taken on sect like leadership behavior where cleansing impure elements from the party has become an obsession with the language of that of a fervent religious diehard: "We should stay alert to the ubiquitous factors that could weaken our Party's pioneering nature and contaminate our Party's purity," he said. "If we don't take strict precautions and correct them in time... small problems will grow into big ones, minor slips will escalate into an irreversible landslide, probably even leading to a broader and subversive catastrophe."[33]

From the CCP perspective, there might be a justified cause of concern in spreading this nationalistic sentiment across the population, various campaigns replacing each other, such as to engage the masses, leading up to the 70th anniversary of the founding of the People's Republic of China, on 1 October 2019. Chinese state media were ordered to drop soap operas and other light entertainment television shows and replace them with patriotic content trying to trigger nationalistic feelings, as there is an obvious concern that its population is not showing enough devotion.[34]

Under the rule of Xi Jinping, now appointed to what in practice is a lifetime leader, the repressive instruments to weed out dissident citizens have been advancing with technological improvements, but at the expense of further mental distress and fatigue, through a sadistically crafted social credit system intended to measure social behavior by a standardized assessment of the economic and social reputation of citizens and businesses, deploying mass surveillance and big data analysis. The harsh repression is starting to show psychological strains on many Chinese, succumbing under the pressure with highlights of mental anguish. In essence, the nightmare of a Big Brother society has for the first time become a reality, with punishments including being publicly blacklisted in a 'name and shame strategy', travel bans and access to hotels, certain types of employment, and even exclusion from elite schools for the children of those with low credit scores.[35]

The party's information machinery is also acting on various social media spreading pro-CCP propaganda, trying to convey the messages it wants its population to adhere to, while also studying public opinion and grievances, and attempting to influence any escalating contentious social issues. Some studies estimate that as many as over two million public opinion analysts, or trolls, and over 800 firms are responsible for public opinion monitoring, a process by some described as *authoritarian deliberation*. Bad news from the perspective of the party are nowadays mostly presented in a way to remove any potential blame from the CCP and the state rather than covering it up as was the previous practice. To make its political propaganda more appealing, it is often intertwined with more light hearted topics such as entertainment and relationship advice, and the offering of winning voucher if one share or re-post their contents to increase engagement from the public. But they sometimes found themselves being mocked, in some cases very creatively, such as likening Xi Jinping to Winnie the Pooh, which have led to any references to the fictitious teddy bear character being banned and censored, highlighting the sensitivity of the regime.[36]

With the economic engine no longer able to deliver the same growth as before, worsened through the only partially settled trade war with the U.S., the government is becoming less able to deliver their part of the bargain. They are concerned that this will be met with more open protests and have acted by pre-empting any grassroot protest movements from taking shape by tightening of controls. The extent of the control apparatus has come to carry the hallmark of paranoia. From a governmental perspective, this control obsession has merits as they know from recent history with the Arab Spring and Color Revolutions in mind, which were triggered by a dissatisfied middle class that had been short-changed on promises that failed to materialize.

These grievances were not exclusively of an economic nature. The instigators of these uprisings often came from the intelligentsia, quite often with a degree from a Western university, and it is important to note that it was not economic doldrums that triggered the unrest in the Middle East and Ukraine, but governments that had become too detached from the realities on the ground. Instead of meeting the concerns of their citizens, they tried to silence them, and bombarded them with shallow propaganda that only accentuated the alienation of the population, prompting aggression in a passive form at first, and eventually taking a more confrontational path.

Herein lies an important insight. The psychological welfare of a population goes above and beyond just economic progress at some point, especially if the citizens have been empowered with a broader perspective on how a relationship between a society and its underlings should really work. In a Maslowian fashion, the opportunity to develop one's individuality and the freedom to choose, including one's own political inclinations, becomes a priority, and once arrived at this level of psychological maturity, no extra financial rewards from the government will suffice as a trade-off.

Turning Xinjiang Into an Open Prison

Some of the party's favorite euphemisms, *stability* and *a harmonious society*, which clearly have Confucian connotations, have come to mean that any challenges to their monopoly of power or questioning of their policies are perceived as threats and must be severely punished. These concepts also take a Han Chinese angle, as the ethnically deviating regions Xinjiang and Tibet, with sizable minorities, have basically turned into open prisons, where re-education and vocational centers (another euphemism for concentration camps and brainwashing facilities) in which forced confessions, through torture, at times televised and broadcasted, are part of the penal system. The concentration camps in Xinjiang were first denied by the Chinese government, but the scale of these unlawful mass detentions, without any court rulings, estimated to hold well above a million prisoners, with plenty of witnesses highlighting sexual violence, systematic torture, and outright murderers, were over time impossible to keep a secret. Beijing then admitted their existence but claimed they were part of an anti-terrorist campaign where Uyghurs, who they argued were at risk of Islamic radicalization, were provided vocational training and rather than prisoners they call them trainees.

But even outside these detention centers strict bans were imposed with regards to a plethora of Islamic practices, and an Orwellian style mass surveillance with cameras and security personnel literally everywhere, turning the region into a de facto prison with forced assimilation. There are no legal protections and, in a true apartheid-style, being of a Uyghur ethnicity is reason enough to be incarcerated. The international outrage has been immense with references to ethnic cleansing and the concentration camps of World War II. The *Uyghur Human Rights Policy Act of 2019* was passed both in the United States Congress and Senate with strong bipartisan support and was met with the usual complaints from China, warning countries to not meddle in their internal affairs.

However, testimonies of even more horrendous activities kept appearing, where in a truly macabre Frankensteinish manner the CCP administered a lucrative trade in removing human organs from prisoners within the penal system and, for a hefty fee, they were offered to both domestic and international patients seeking heart transplants and other procedures requiring spare human body parts. Whereas patients usually have to wait for years to find suitable organs, all it took for human transplant tourists was to book a time at a clinic in China and then commence the procedure. Complaints and rumors had been around for years, mainly from Falun Gong supporters, but had been brushed off as sensationalist fantasies. The stories came across as too grotesque, too monstrous to be true. Eventually, a tribunal was set up, *The Independent Tribunal into Forced Organ Harvesting from Prisoners of Conscience in China,* led by Sir Geoffrey Nice, a seasoned barrister with a background investigating crimes against human rights, including in Syria and Yugoslavia. They arrived at the conclusion that there is extensive evidence that China has been killing prisoners on a substantial scale, including prisoners of conscience, to remove organs for commercial human transplantation. The tribunal concluded that:

> Forced organ harvesting has been committed for years through China on a significant scale and that Falun Gong practitioners have been one—and probably the main source of organ supply. The concerted persecution and medical testing of the Uyghurs is more recent and it may be that evidence of forced organ harvesting of this group may emerge in due course.[37]

Cracks Appearing in the Wall...

The protests in Hong Kong have not go unnoticed by many mainland Chinese, as there are around one million relatively recent immigrants from China in Hong Kong that either remained silent or joined the protest movement. Throughout the crisis they have brought back to family and friends in China significantly different insights than what the Chinese media have tried to convey. It was also not lost on them that, through pro-active social media exposure, clever demonstration tactics, and international pressure, the mighty CCP budged and dared not venture to undertake a full-scale violent crackdown by sending in troops. The local government was forced to withdraw the hated extradition bill. The old truth proved again to be correct, transparency scares dictators and prevents them from committing atrocities.

Cracks in the wall are starting to appear, social media protests against imposed restrictions on free speech in some of the leading colleges have been noted and, for China, are unusually vocal. Tertiary education includes compulsory classes on the long since anachronistic Marxist theory and has more recently been supplemented by something that appears equally dated, labelled *Xi Jinping's Thoughts on Socialism with Chinese Characteristics for a New Era*. It is a collection of statements, and, for a document intended to inspire, it is surprisingly bland, that promotes the party's authority domestically and the attempts to ensure China's place in the world as a great nation. Also, many otherwise party-loyal academics have raised concern against the heavy politicization of universities as it aspires to harmonize thoughts and opinions and hampers creativity and innovation.

With the outbreak of the coronavirus in early 2020, with its pandemic epicenter in Wuhan and the Hebei province, the CCP's demand to control all information again has led to widespread complaints, as early information of a potential virus outbreak was covered-up. Many remembered how the government had gone to great lengths to sweep the SARS outbreak in 2003 under the carpet. It highlights the intrinsic weakness with a dictatorship's monopoly on the information flow, as it insists that there can only be one version of reality, theirs, which means extensively filtering and vehemently rejecting a free debate.

The result which also should be obvious to the CCP, is that many will distrust it, especially in a life and death situation which a virus outbreak is, thus various rumors will come to flourish, and as the government tries to silence these, it will raise further suspicions. Implicitly, many Chinese come to realize that the CCP comes first, not the people.

In the case of the coronavirus, it was at first covered-up by local leaders who did not want to deliver bad news to Beijing, being accused of not maintaining social stability and causing panic, which led to the critical initial time to contain the virus and prevent it from becoming a pandemic being lost. Being the harbinger of bad news in a dictatorship, which might or might not in hindsight be correct, is something best avoided. One of the first whistle blowers, Dr. Li Wenliang, who succumbed to the virus after having contracted it in the Wuhan Hospital he worked at, was summoned by the Public Security Bureau, accused of making false comments and severely disturbing the social order by issuing warnings about the severity of the virus. He was forced, like others that early on raised concerns, to sign a letter of confession. He is now remembered in China for what are remembered as his passing words, "A healthy society should not only have one voice." China's censorship of news has made the country fertile ground for rumors, as people do not trust official information. The CCP allowed the virus to spread to become a worldwide pandemic, and forced China to take draconian measures to contain it.

The Uneasy Relationship Between China and the World

To position China as an emerging global power on the world stage has become a priority for the CCP, summed up in the slogan, "Deng Xiaoping made us rich, now Xi Jinping is making us strong." But it has been noted by many that the Chinese charm offensive with the world is not quite working. It might be a matter of temperament, as Chinese diplomats often come across as too rigorous and too harsh, with a noted lack of willingness to seek win-win solutions. There is now a strong sentiment in the world that China operates using predatory trade practices, which it backs up with heavy-handed politics, trying to force its counterparts using coercion, threatening them with various types of boycotts and at times publicly resorting to outright black mail.

Its venture into the South China Sea, with an artificial island that has been militarized and territorial claims disputed by all its neighbors and rejected by an international court, has acerbated the view of China as a ruthless brute clamping down on the rights of smaller nations, operating on a might is right principle and a disdain for international rules and human rights. China's previous goodwill as an up and coming nation has notably receded and has now reversed into a general distrust, something which President Trump has cleverly used to the advantage of the United States in turning China into the world's bad boy.

In this context, it is surprising that the world's largest political party, with huge resources at its disposal to monitor the sentiments of the population, acts so psychologically clumsy, almost naïve in its world view. This clumsiness extends to its foreign language media, such as *China Daily*, *Global Times*, and other mouth pieces that target an international audience by providing a Chinese perspective. Western observers are often astonished by the highly arcane, even hysterical, language used by the Chinese authorities when they wish to vent their anger and resentment, often referring to "the hurt feelings of the Chinese people."

This drastic language is often given a historical reference, with the so-called "century of humiliation" leading up to the first half of the twentieth century, with the Opium Wars, the Boxer Uprising, and the Japanese Occupation as reference points. By using such excessively strong language appears to signal that China never again would allow itself to be dominated by foreign powers.

To an international audience, its actual intent is often misinterpreted, and leaves the Western reader baffled. They are often unsure if there is some hidden sarcasm, as the draconian language appears so extreme, not used to prose void of nuances, zealous in its vocabulary dividing the world in good and evil, deploying hell fire rhetoric when throwing out accusations of evil and wickedness. It is somehow remarkable that they do not realize that such language completely fails to resonate with its intended audience. It appears weird, even farcical, like the vocabulary of a person that cannot quite grasp what is going on and keeps reacting out-of-tune. It becomes evident that they lack the resources to handle individuals groomed in a pluralistic society capable of comprehending divergent views and ambiguities.

The contrast with an authoritarian worldview becomes evident as the dogma is so embedded in their political doctrine that any deviation must be met in very harsh terms. Often these English language communiques are almost direct translations from Chinese. This to ensure the party line is strictly maintained. Hence, a Western observer can obtain insight as to how the worldview of CCP devotees is defined, or at least, an idea of how they believe it should work. It also highlights how meagre the public discourse becomes in such an authoritarian society, where a plethora of varying, even distinctly contrasting views are not allowed to co-exist. In fact, through studying the party program, it almost becomes possible to create algorithms on given responses to any political issues and queries. It has become a lifeless ritualized discourse, where no dynamics or unexpected events must be allowed for, which is, of course, an impossibility in the real messy world.

The standard reply to defuse any criticism has been the default comment of hurting the feelings of the Chinese population and expecting that comment to end the discussion in CCP's favor. This no longer works. The more aggressive stance by China in the world arena has exposed the falsity of their claim that solely the CCP can speak for the Chinese people, and that their arguments are shared by the population in its entirety. That narrative is being increasingly rejected. The CCP is the current dictatorial regime of mainland China, and through extreme repression clamps down on any deviating views, but Chinese culture and Chinese people, both residing in or outside mainland China, are very different concepts indeed, and do not overlap other than in minor segments. They are now having a much more difficult time to defuse difficult and pointed questions by referring to being the sole representative for the Chinese and Chinese culture, as it is rebuffed as nonsense.

The Chinese leadership tends only to speak of the economic aspects of globalization but rarely, if ever, mentions political global standards, often becoming uneasy, even hysterically hostile, when human rights are mentioned. For an aspiring global leader, China has not managed to build any deeper friendship with other countries, as suspicion on both sides, and a general distrust of China's ulterior motives, prevents it. The international arena consists of a plethora of views, healthy disagreements, plenty of criticism, and sometimes witty sarcasms as part of open debate, an intellectual milieu that representatives for China in the various forums feel highly uncomfortable with. They are unable to handle critique and transparency, as it is alien to what is going on in the Chinese public discourse, where closed doors and excessive restriction of information only allow the single voice of the party, and anything outside of that is deemed illegal.

Herein lies a key point that is now sinking in with the CCP's leadership. They need the world more than the world needs them. China is having great difficulties in demonstrating the allure of their societal model that tolerates no differing political views, with authorities cracking down with brutality on any signs of opposition. Severe abuse of human rights simply does not go down well, especially amongst the tech-savvy millennial generation that seeks to define themselves through exploring their individuality, no matter what form that might take. China has come to realize, to its great embarrassment, how isolated they are in the world when they have tried to present their side of the story about the Hong Kong crisis. Apart from unwavering support from North Korea, they have garnered little support elsewhere, and what is worse is that the unfolding events in Hong Kong have opened the eyes of many to the control-obsessed police-state and the abuse of human rights that is the Chinese model of governance. There are simply no politicians in the West that openly support China, even though they do likely have some of them on their payroll as lobbyists, but they also remain silent.

Ideologically, the CCP of today, unlike that of its past under the leadership of Mao Tse Tung, have little to offer in terms of political visions that can inspire. Chairman Mao claimed to lead a revolutionary movement that aspired to build a worker's paradise, a society void of economic classes where equality reigned, also between genders, a political dream that won quite a few supporters in the left-wing student movement of the 1960s, not only in the West, but also in many Third World countries.

The existing political cadre of the CCP are far from revolutionaries driven by idealism that want to develop a socialist utopia. It is instead showing hallmarks of becoming a kleptocracy, where most in the leadership have used their political influence to develop vast business interests that has made many of them billionaires, made possible through nepotism, corruption, and shady deals enabled through a judicial system where legal decisions always goes in favor of the one with best political contacts. Political ideals based simply on enriching themselves and clinging to power at all costs just do not resonate with existing political movements that hold sway outside China. The CCP is therefore not seen as providing an enticing political ideology inspiring people to work for a better and more human world.

Its failure to understand the inner workings of a pluralistic world has, when proactively confronted by it, ignited the CCP's old reactionary patterns in dealing with foreigners: suspicion, xenophobia, and clumsy attempts to brush over events that do not correspond with the image they want to promote. These attitudes hardly facilitate their aspirations on the world arena, which has been duly noticed by the international community, concluding that their attitude is simply too insular and too awkward to be able to provide transparent and enticing global leadership.

Chapter 5

Hong Kong, the Spark that Started a Prairie Fire?

"A single spark can start a prairie fire."

> — Mao Tse Tung (January 5, 1930),
> *Selected Works*, Vol. I, p. 119.

Hong Kong has, since 1997 when the United Kingdom handed it back to China, been regulated under a 50-year agreement, where a one country, two systems model applies that provides for a certain political autonomy for the former crown colony. Yet the question of truly free democratic elections was left hanging. A similar arrangement was made with the then-neighboring Portuguese colony of Macau in 1999, although in practice that was immediately scrapped with Beijing taking full control over the political administration. For Hong Kong, however, this agreement has largely been upheld and respected by China until the last few years, as, unlike Macau mainly acting as a gambling cum money laundering hub, Hong Kong has been useful to them as a financial center to raise funds in a convertible currency, the Hong Kong dollar, which the domestic financial centers in Shanghai and Shenzhen are unable to do. But the CCP leadership was never comfortable with the two systems part of the deal, as it meant that there were and remain aspects of Hong Kong that are not under the full control of the party. As a result, they have recently made attempts to reel these in, which have met with public dissatisfaction.

The increased political pressure from the mainland in withdrawing civic liberties are, however, only a part of the many adversities and lack of freedoms that Hong Kongers have to face. Strange as it might seem, Hong Kong is a place that has for decades been lauded as the world's freest economy, with low, in fact hardly any taxes nor unemployment, a mere 2.8 percent unemployed prior to the commencement of the unrest, according to the Census and Statistics Department. The state coffers are bloated by surplus cash, which would make most other economies envious. It also rates as Asia's leading financial and travel hub, with a world class infrastructure. However, scratching below the surface, there are a number of escalating issues that together with the removal of political freedoms are causing distress and leading to a radicalization of large segments of the population.

Despite the claim that Hong Kong is one of the world's freest economies, it is an open secret that most of its industries operate through oligopolies, where a few families are controlling most key business sectors, guarding themselves jealously, through political connections and a biased legal system, against any newcomers trying to challenge them. Tourists visiting the low-tax jurisdiction of Hong Kong are often surprised that the general price levels of goods and services rarely are below (and not infrequently even higher) than those of their own high-tax societies. The reason for the artificially high prices, despite Hong Kong not having a sales tax, is explained through the numerous cartels that exist in most business sectors, in addition to the exorbitantly high rents, as much of the property sector is also controlled by a handful of tycoons. This creates a sort of hidden tax that ends up lining their pockets, rather than the riches being distributed throughout society. And it is hard, if not impossible, to go about life in Hong Kong without in some way enriching these tycoons.

Not only do these cartels charge the consumers excessive prices, given the lack of competition, but they also operate inefficiently. Foreigners visiting any bank branch in Hong Kong will often find themselves in a 1980s time capsule, where fax is still routinely used for communication, checks still a common means of payment, and the number of bank clerks are four to five times higher than in any equivalent bank branch in Europe or the United States. Any complaints about cartel formations and price fixing to the local Hong Kong politicians never lead anywhere and grievances from the general population are as a rule ignored. The reason for this can be found in Hong Kong's peculiar political system with its functional constituencies, where the business sector (read: the tycoons) controls a disproportionate number of seats in the legislative council and electoral committee, and without their support no reforms are possible.

Hong Kong is without any effective consumer-friendly legislations, like anti-trust laws, and the few that have been introduced are so watered down that they lack the desired effect. In their absence, business arrangements such as price fixing, which have long been strictly regulated in jurisdictions like the U.S. and E.U., can continue to operate freely with detrimental consequences to consumers. These arrangements which have produced excessive profits for decades, to use some Marxist parlance, have made the tycoons extremely rich, with most of them qualifying for Forbes' billionaires list. The resignation of a Hong Kong tycoon usually means his demise or a medical deterioration leading to a demented or vegetative state. With many of these first generation's tycoons now in their late 80s and above, a generational shift is occurring, but unlike that of American and European self-made men, like Warren Buffet or the late Swedish furniture magnate Ingvar Kamprad, when realizing the leadership limitations or disinterest of their offspring, they will nominate an outsider to eventually take over, for a traditional Chinese family such arrangements are almost unthinkable.

The eldest son must, competent or not, take over, being truly nepotistic family-run empires distancing themselves from society at large.

The most well-known of these tycoons, Li Ka Shing who, up until recently, headed his flagship conglomerate CK Hutchison Holdings, now run by his eldest son, through it and its affiliate companies, he economically impacts most aspects of a Hong Konger's everyday life. It spans from the properties they live, work, and shop in, to the electricity consumed, the telecom network used, as well as the pharmacy, drugstore, and supermarket goods they consume. Li Ka Shing's career is the typical tell-tale story, shared by most acclaimed rags-to-riches tycoons, that according to corporate legend began building his business empire by producing plastic flowers, eventually moving in to property investments, buying them dirt cheap during the political unrest in the 1960s, and in the late 1970s. He took over a faltering business conglomerate through benevolent financial support from HSBC, Hong Kong's leading bank throughout its history. He became the then-crown colony's first Chinese boss of one of the famous trading companies, the *Hongs*. Most of these deals highlighted an astuteness in picking up assets and companies on the cheap, and within only a few years, through proactive measures, seeing their values increase greatly. For a long time, the business acumen of Li Ka Shing, as well as his fellow tycoons, was widely admired by the Hong Kong population. He was referred to as "Superman," a role model for every young aspiring businessman. Hard work, outsmarting the competition, sponsoring the token charity event, and golf as the rare leisure activity, were the modus operandi for any would-be Superman. But there have not really been any new up and coming Supermen ready to replace this now hastily demising generation with the average age of a Hong Kong billionaire being in the late 80s, this as most business sectors keep out any newcomers through their oligopoly structure. This fact, together with the insight that most of the tycoons' riches come at the expense of the Hong Kong population, and that they have done little in terms of corporate social responsibility, have led over time to their declining popularity that now stands at an all-time low.

The extraordinarily unequal society that has evolved is taking its toll on living conditions, where apartments of a closet size routinely sell for around 1 million USD, and even well-educated youngsters are forced to live with their parents until their mid-30s, making marriages and family formation difficult. The inequality, as measured by the Gini index, is equivalent to any Third World country. The legislated minimum wage is only 4.75 USD per hour, simply impossible to sustain a household on. It is estimated that about 1.4 million live below poverty line, almost 20 percent of the population, often living in subdivided flats, with the average living space for a Hong Konger being only about 10 square feet. Little has been done to alleviate their poverty, as interest from mainstream politicians to do so has basically been non-existent.

This unwillingness by the government to rectify socio-economic inequality has increasingly fueled a sense of animosity and hopelessness, where many feel that they are being robbed of the opportunity for a decent life. Beijing has failed to give the Hong Kong grassroots class hope by remaining silent through its puppet politicians for decades. The political system is under the almost complete control of the local tycoons and pro-Beijing elements and addressing inequality issues has not been on their agenda. For a regime, that in name at least defines itself as communist, it has, ironically, throughout its control over Hong Kong, sided with the business elite rather than the proletariat. Many leading members of the CCP have close business relationships with the tycoons, and own considerable assets in Hong Kong, both real estate and interests in listed companies.

Since the handover in 1997, the level of economic inequalities has worsened and there have been several protest movements taking to the streets, given their denial of parliamentary representation. The Umbrella protest movement that erupted in 2014, in addition to their demands for Western-style democracy, took aim at the business practices of these tycoons and their crony politicians, labelling them as robber barons, one of the least offensive slogans in these protests. There was a preceding Occupy Central movement in 2011-2012 that also voiced dissatisfaction against economic and social injustice. Other previous protests also contained a mixture of protest against both withdrawn human rights and economic inequalities. Similarly, there was a 2012 proposal that would have required students to receive patriotic education, which also was withdrawn after being fiercely rejected by large scale street protests as an attempt at brainwashing. Theses recurring street protests since the handover have become the means to vent anger and frustration against proposed policies as the Hong Kong government has severely restricted political rights, such as jailing pro-democracy activists and imposing limitations on who could run for office. The government has also enforced a blanket ban on political parties that advocate independence.

The proposed introduction of the extradition bill in early 2019, although sugar coated as intended to comply with international standards, was intended to avoid the bad press China was receiving from kidnapping political dissidents in Hong Kong, of which some had foreign citizenships, albeit being of mainland Chinese origin, as well as using it as a threat to silence political protests in Hong Kong. China demanded its usually compliant pro-Beijing Legislative Council majority, that typically never deviates from what the CCP orders them to do, to pass this extradition bill. But even some of the pro-Beijing politicians started to hesitate as they realized the scope of the bill which would put any Hong Kong resident, including foreigners staying in Hong Kong, even if only as tourists, that somehow had caught the anger of the CCP, at risk of an extradition request from mainland China. There they could be exposed to trumped up charges, usually not related to the perceived political offence they were accused of, completely void of any genuine legal assistance. They can be accused of corruption, tax evasion, or a whole raft of other fabricated offences, even traffic violations, just to get them into the penal system where they typically are subject to torture and forced confessions. The bill also allowed for the freezing of any assets held in Hong Kong pending investigation. Above and beyond the bill being a tool for political repression, it was also feared that it could extend to business disputes, where mainland counterparts affiliated with the CCP could concoct charges against its Hong Kong based business partners, call for their extradition, and put them in front of a partial court, freeze their assets, and in effect confiscate their business interests.

The foreign chambers of commerce in Hong Kong protested in an unusually vocal manner, and even the Hong Kong Chamber of Commerce, with its tycoons known to rarely contradict edicts from the local CCP cronies, also echoed concerns, albeit in milder terms. They knew that the introduction of such an extradition bill would mean the end of Hong Kong as a commercial center, because Hong Kong would no longer be seen as a safe gateway into China if the long arm of the mainland Chinese politicized law enforcement and judicial system would extend its reach into the territory. What was worse, politicians from both the U.S. and the European Union started to indicate that they might revoke Hong Kong's special trade status, which has made it exempted from the U.S. trade tariffs. Thus, from an international perspective, Hong Kong would be treated like any other city in China, which would be a devastating blow for its dominant finance and property sectors.

Under such circumstances, the Legislative Council started to blink, a sentiment underpinned by unprecedented public protests, estimated at around two million taking to the streets to protest against the extradition bill on 16 June 2019, an extraordinary number in a city of 7.4 million, even though the Chief Executive, Carrie Lam Cheng Yuet-ngor, had announced that she was withdrawing the bill a day earlier. Carrie Lam is a life-long bureaucrat with a noted lack of capability to connect with people and notorious for her arrogant attitude. Referring herself as a devout Catholic, she often implicitly declares that she represents divine forces in her work as Chief Executive. A baffling claim, as she has been an unwavering supporter of the CCP, notorious for persecuting Christians, including underground Catholics, destroying churches, and engaging in other religious clamp downs. Regardless of her proclaimed religious devotion, it was not more deep-rooted than she being part of the Beijing pre-selected candidates that were allowed to run for the office of chief executive, where loyalty rather than capability is the key selection criteria. Her political and human touch shortcomings have greatly exacerbated the crisis, an insight not lost on Beijing, which have been forced to support her throughout the crisis so as not to appear to be swayed by popular opinion. And she was shortly after the large scale protests seen crying and sulking at a press conference where she complained how she had been misunderstood by the public. After that, she has in effect gone into hiding, making only occasional public appearances to make insipid comments as per instructions from Beijing.

Throughout the summer of 2019, the protests evolved from the initial demands to withdraw the extradition bill, to include a broader spectrum of democratic rights, such as universal suffrage, and extending to slogans such as "Free Hong Kong," with widespread street protests being hailed by some of the demonstrators as an "era of revolution." Slogans demanding independence have obviously triggered strong reactions from Beijing and was designed to be provocative in order to escalate matters where the mainland authorities had little choice but to bring in troops, risking an outright civil war. The protests of 2019, in comparison to previous demonstrations, have been much more far-ranging and included storming the Legislative Council, shutting down the airport, and disrupting public transports, events that have been met by excessive police violence, where a record number of tear gas canisters have been unleashed, even inside train stations, and with the law enforcement seen working in cahoots with triads to attack demonstrators.

The protestor's frustrations and disappointments have, in part, turned from Carrie Lam and her government to the CCP itself. On 21 July 2019, there was a protest against Beijing's Central Government Liaison Office in Hong Kong, where the state seal of China was pelted with eggs and black paint, a direct confrontation as state symbols are regarded almost as religious icons and any insulting behavior towards them are seen as blasphemy, acts that risk of long prison sentences. Complaints from the other signatory of the handover agreement, which is set to expire in 2047, the United Kingdom, suggested that the rights and freedoms set down in the Sino-British Joint Declaration should be upheld, were met defiantly by the Foreign Ministry in Beijing, accusing Britain of "grossly interfering in Hong Kong affairs" and declaring the handover agreement is in effect void, as it "no longer has any practical significance."

Interestingly, the scale of the protests came as the proverbial lighting striking out of a blue sky for both the Hong Kong government and the Central Government Liaison Office, simply bewildered at the magnitude and degree of anger from the population. This in itself is a surprise as Beijing has long seen Hong Kong as a potential hotbed for dissident activities. The Canton province (Guangdong) traditionally has been an origin of revolutionary tendencies, most notably with Sun Yat Sen involved in events that eventually led to the overthrow of the Emperor in 1911. Thus, Beijing has over the years spent considerable resources setting up networks to collect intelligence trying to get a feel for the mood and political sentiments of Hong Kongers. However, both Carrie Lam's government, which is required to be in constant communication with the CCP to take instructions, as well as Beijing's own information and intelligence bodies, appear to have had no insight of the protests that were to unfold, nor an understanding of the pent-up anger that had been building up among large segments of the population. Only a month prior to the protests, Vice-Premier Han Zheng, the CCP's man in charge of Hong Kong and Macau affairs, informed the National Congress that "the political atmosphere in Hong Kong is changing for the better" and "Hong Kong has set on to the right path of development."

So, what is the likely reason for the poor understanding of the mood of the general public? It is due to a combination of factors, the typical authoritarian phenomena of the yes sayers' syndrome is playing out, where no one wants to deliver perceived bad news, as that can be regarded as an indirect critique to the leadership with an overhanging risk of being exposed to a "shoot the messenger" career ending move. But it also comes down to a mindset that has been castrated through a lifelong marination in a very narrow black and white world view, where anything that deviates from the party line, is simply psychologically disregarded and not actually grasped, much like the partial blindness of the Emperor's New Clothes condition. Diverging views are simply seen as aberrations, ideas only held by a miniscule minority, and therefore not worthy of being taken seriously. But the psychological mechanisms at work in an authoritarian mindset are rarely considered as causal factors to intelligence blunders. Instead, experts blame the failure on organizational dysfunctions among the information and intelligence gathering agencies that has led to a lack of coherent analysis and coordination. Hence, the frustration and disappointment that erupted into street protests, with the radicalization of the middle class, supporting even the storming of the Legislative Council and the occupation of the airport, were never factored in as a plausible scenario because of this highly lopsided mind-set.

But even if they had been able to foresee it, and pre-empt some of the protests by imposing curfews, or even introducing the Emergency Regulations Ordinance that provides the Chief Executive with dictatorial powers, it might likely only have further infuriated Hong Kongers who never have been shy of speaking their mind, and instead triggered anger to reach boiling point and erupted in large scale violence. Even with an accurate insight into the majority of Hong Kongers' political sentiments, as these so distinctly contravene the doctrine of the CCP, an open dialogue to seek common ground through compromise would still be unlikely as Beijing seeks absolute obedience from its subjects.

The CCP and Hong Kong government's inability to communicate with its citizens has not gone unnoticed. President Trump sent a mocking tweet during the crisis, urging Xi Jinping to go and meet the protestors in Hong Kong in order to solve the crisis, knowing very well that their Achilles' heel is their inability to communicate with the general public, and being able to argue convincingly against political opinions that differs against their own. Hong Kong is simply a case in point on how badly the government understands the needs and psychological well-being of its citizens.[38]

Whilst the handover now lies more than 20 years in the past, Hong Kongers and mainland Chinese have not been able to get closer and harmonize their mindsets and personalities. In part, it is a language issue. In the southern Guangdong province, Cantonese is mainly spoken, whilst the lingua franca promoted in China is Mandarin. Attempts to communicate simultaneously using the two languages, not dialects, are virtually unintelligible, with Hong Kongers not infrequently praising themselves for their poor Mandarin language skills. But ethnically they share a common background. Hong Kong, after World War II, had only had about half a million inhabitants, compared to today's 7.4 million, of which about 92 percent are of (mainly Han) Chinese origin. This means that for most families, their links to mainland China only go back one or two generations, with about one million arriving from the mainland over the last 25 years. Most fled the horrors of communism and have first-hand experiences of the atrocities, duress, and massacres a communist dictatorial society can impose on its citizens. It is in a sense ironic that many of the pro-Beijing politicians in Hong Kong are first generation descendants of those that fled China in search of safety, freedom, and a better life. Their parents provided them with, in comparison, a privileged life, free from the prospect of dying of starvation, a very tangible risk in China in those days, and being granted freedoms, such as being allowed to have more than one child, freedom of speech, and other civic liberties that would have been denied them if their parents had remained in China. However, this irony takes a tragic twist as the very privileges that their parents once bestowed upon them by fleeing to Hong Kong, and fully exploited, they are now seeking to withdraw from the younger generation.

This shameless hypocrisy is one of the sources for the exploding anger in Hong Kong. It has caused a rift between generations. This as the many of the middle aged and elderly are satisfied with their material well-being, having experienced an affluent easy life that saw Hong Kong go through unprecedented growth from the 1960s onwards that made many of them millionaires by simply buying a couple of modest apartments in what used to be working class areas, but are now gentrified and have multiplied in price many times over. This economic windfall has created a bloated comfortable rentier class, with little other focus in life than voluptuous eating and extravagant holidays. To them, safeguarding their privileges by not rocking the boat is prioritized over giving the young generation the chance to prosper and safeguard their political rights, however limited. Many of them, already materially satisfied, have, therefore, remained indifferent to the prospect of Hong Kong being fully integrated under Chinese repression.

In contrast, stands the younger generation, better educated, with an international perspective, but for which it has almost become an impossibility to enter the property ladder with only closet size apartments sold at extortion prices on offer, in comparison to the relatively sizable public estates provided for the impoverished generations in the 1970s. A not unjustified feeling of unfairness has gained ground among them. With economic opportunities no longer being as easily accessible as before, even when equipped with a university degree, the sense of hopelessness has been on the increase, a sentiment this young generation is to some degree sharing with their contemporaries on the mainland. Part of it has, of course, to do with structural changes about which politicians of any conviction can do little. Ongoing automation is transforming the economy into a knowledge-based economy, with the introduction of robots and artificial intelligence now even in high-end service sectors which are reducing the number of possible entry level positions. It is making career prospects even worse for those with little or no education, and the hope of ever becoming financially self-sufficient has become a pipe dream.

With local politicians putting further pressure on the young generation by threatening to take away the last of the few political freedoms that have remained, has forced many into radicalization. It is simply that few people who have grown up in a free society voluntarily would like to live in an authoritarian state. To Hong Kongers, it is reflected in their worst fear, to become just another Chinese city. The support for the protests against the extradition bill et. al. has been overwhelming, while the few and far between pro-government demonstrations only manage to gather a fraction of supporters in comparison. This is highly worrying for the CCP, especially given the fact that so many mainland immigrants now live in the city, who have been educated and indoctrinated in pro-CCP propaganda throughout the educational system, but openly show so little support for it when these ideological tenets are being publicly confronted. The broad majority of these mainland immigrants have not been seen out on the streets voicing their support for the local government or Beijing. They have, by-and-large, remained silent or joined the pro-democracy movement, sometimes publicly so.

This insight is sending shivers down the spine as the CCP is forced to recognize on what thin ground their claim to power rests. The dogma imposed on mainland Chinese who have emigrated is obviously being questioned to the point of no longer openly endorsing it, and often passively rejected, when their legitimacy is challenged in a pluralistic society. Hence, when exposed to a more open world, the ideological basis of the very one-sided educational system, often referred to as outright brainwashing, appears to fade quickly. A disturbing and frightening insight to the CCP, when realizing how fragile is the general public's loyalty to it.[39]

At the time of the handover in 1997, Hong Kong was of great importance to the Chinese economy, being far more sophisticated, especially in terms of the financial industry. This importance has faded over time, and today Hong Kong's contribution to the Chinese economy is estimated to be only a couple of percent of the total GDP, dropping from over 20 percent. Its population stands at only about half a percent of the total population, however their GDP per capita is about five times that of the mainland Chinese. But Hong Kong still holds some pivotal key advantages that mainland China cannot yet, if ever, match. Many investors in China prefer to use Hong Kong-based legal contracts because they are still regulated by a British-style common law judicial system, unlike China's legal system which is routinely influenced by political pressure to reach a certain verdict, or so corrupted that verdicts will favor the best paying claimant. Also, the convertible status of the Hong Kong dollar vis-à-vis the Renminbi provides a distinct advantage, funds can easily be exchanged and withdrawn, something which is far from always is the case in mainland China. To list a company on the Hong

Kong Stock Exchange is also a way to raise foreign currency, which is not possible on the mainland stock exchanges. Many of these deals involve senior and well-connected members of the CCP, a financial incentive they are unwilling to lose, which would happen if Hong Kong's special trade status should be revoked by the U.S. and E.U. as a protest against increasing Chinese political meddling in Hong Kong's affairs.[40]

After the Burning Summer of 2019, What is Next for Hong Kong?

As the burning summer of 2019 ended with the extradition bill withdrawn but no other concessions made by a government remaining as aloof and tone deaf as ever to its population's concerns, Carrie Lam's regime held out futile hopes for protest fatigue. The government hoped for a similar outcome as the Occupy Central events in 2014, where eventually the revolutionary fervor of the protestors faded, and the general public's support started to wane given the inconvenience the demonstrations and other grassroots protests caused to everyday life. Back then, it simply led to things returning relatively quickly to the previous unhappy situation, with none of the underlying problems resolved. Political repression and economic inequality continued. This scenario would be the least costly for the government, at least in the short term, as it counted on an implicit acceptance of status quo. This would allow them, within a few years, to try to re-introduce something akin to the scrapped extradition bill.

To this point, the government has heavily emphasized the damaging impact the protests were having on the local economy. Although the protests scared away tourists, mainly from the mainland, which has hurt hotels, the food and beverage sector, as well as luxury retail businesses, in reality, the Hong Kong economy had already started to slow a couple of quarters prior to the commencement of the protests, this due in part to the trade war, but also because the Chinese economy domestically was no longer growing at the same pace as before. Of course, the protests exacerbated this downturn and have made many international firms consider Hong Kong's future viability as a regional hub. But had the government succeeded in passing the extradition bill, the economic consequences would been much worse, as the mainland Chinese legal system would have, in effect, extended to Hong Kong, and exposed international firms to the possibility of black mail and repercussions from the CCP, an unpleasant insight not lost on the foreign chambers of commerce, but one that Carrie Lam and her government were numb about.

There was also a genuine fear that Beijing's patience would come to an end and that it would send in armed forces from the People's Liberation Army (PLA). There was indeed saber-rattling throughout the summer with film clips being released of troop concentrations close to the border. However, in the end, they never did so. There are a number of reasons for this; throughout the protests there were cameras everywhere and film clips of the local police force's excessive violence were instantly posted on social media. Any more serious atrocities committed by the PLA would have been relayed to the world instantly, and with the sensitive trade negotiations with the U.S. ongoing, they would become a political impossibility from the U.S. perspective. Various types of boycotts – commercial, political, and cultural – could also be expected from the world community, even putting the 2022 Beijing Olympics at risk. Such a forceful PLA crackdown, given the massive support of the protesters by the population, could easily also have escalated into guerrilla style street fighting were military causalities are likely to have become significant, as the PLA lacks combat experience. It would also have contradicted the CCP's claim that the demonstrators were merely a small minority under the command of sinister foreign forces. Eventually, it could have required a full-scale occupation at enormous financial costs and immense practical difficulties, likely leading to the public engaging in general strikes and lockdown of the city. What maybe was practically possible, was politically impossible, a calculation that the CCP arrived at.

For Beijing, the censorship of the events in Hong Kong to its domestic audience has been excessive, trying to frame it as a challenge to China's sovereignty, rather than a pro-democracy movement. It has openly blamed a foreign conspiracy for instigating trouble and coercing the young generation into causing disorder, asserting that the protestors are merely a small minority of the Hong Kong population. As autumn arrived, the protests became, with a few exceptions, less frequent and smaller in scale, however splinter groups resorted to more violent tactics, something akin to a Baader Meinhof-like urban guerrilla movement where petrol bombs, even bows and arrows, became the standard arsenal in fights with the police force. The Hong Kong police force, previously known as Asia's finest and held in highest esteem, was now regarded as an instrument of tyranny under the direct control of Beijing. The police were ordered to crush anyone that stood up for human rights. And despite documented evidence of excessive violence, and accusations of both torture and sexual abuse, they have so far remained above the law.

A mantra that the government kept repeating throughout the summer, was that a silent majority sided with them and actually supported the introduction of the extradition bill, a myth that was dispelled through the district council elections held on the 24 November 2019, where pro-Beijing candidates lost control of 17 out of 18 district council seats, and pro-democracy forces won 388 of 452 district council seats. The election had a record turnout. 71% of the registered voters turned up to vote, in total 57% voted for various pro-democracy candidates, and 42% for pro-Beijing candidates. Whilst district councilors mainly focus on matters such as garbage collection and provision of public facilities in their specific areas and have little political sway to influence national legislation, this election was viewed as a referendum on the government's policies and performance. In all, it was crushing defeat for Carrie Lam and became an exercise in eating humble pie for Beijing, which remained silent about the actual outcome in its domestic news reporting. CCP's claim that it solely can define what political views that any Chinese must subscribe to was obliterated by the Hong Kong electorate, and so far, the government has carried on like nothing happened, which has further infuriated Hong Kongers and kept adding to rather than reducing their many resentments. From an international perspective, this was framed as a David versus Goliath struggle and the demonstrators stood on moral high ground as freedom fighters for a just cause, despite some more fanatical elements causing ugly scenes of vandalism and violence, some with a deadly outcome.

The detrimental international public relation disaster that the incompetent handling of the protests was causing appears to, at least outwardly, have been completely lost on both Carrie Lam's government and Beijing which simply kept parroting platitudes about foreign interference and the demand for national security at all costs. The protests were labelled by the government as solely an internal affair, and they warned foreign politicians and international bodies from interfering, however much in vain. Political pressure was building up as human rights organizations, such as Amnesty International, issued strong condemnations of the excessive police violence.

In a rare moment of unity since Donald Trump became president, there was bipartisan consensus in amending the United States-Hong Kong Policy Act of 1992 that passed both houses of Congress in record time. The Hong Kong Human Rights and Democracy Act 2019 means that the U.S. Secretary of State will have to certify whether Hong Kong remains, "sufficiently autonomous to justify special treatment by the

United States... including the degree to which Hong Kong's autonomy has been eroded due to actions taken by the Government of China." It provides far reaching possibilities to freeze the U.S.-based assets of, and deny entry to the U.S. by, any individual deemed responsible for violating human rights in Hong Kong.

In a sense, what the CCP aspired to do, albeit somewhat covertly, namely making Hong Kong into just another city in China by extending its long arm of the law, this fait accompli becoming recognized abroad, and any special agreements that have provided Hong Kong with special favors vis-à-vis China will soon be a thing of the past. In that light, complaints by Carrie Lam and her regime are futile, as they themselves sow the seeds of what more and more starts to look like the beginning of the end for Hong Kong.

Beijing Kills the Two Systems

The resolve and tenacity of the Hong Kong population has, throughout the crisis, been grossly underestimated by pretty much all external observers, as has the magnitude of the support, given the broad public participation. It has triggered a political embarrassment for Beijing that it has a hard time handling, coming across as bully with no respect for human rights. Mainland Chinese media has been broadcasting the protests through highly selective images, well-chosen to try to stir up public opinion against the demonstrators, using vocabulary such as 'treachery' and 'terrorism'. But the majority of the protestors accept, sometimes unwillingly for purely pragmatic reasons, Beijing's sovereign claim over Hong Kong, and merely seek to maintain its relatively freer way of life compared to the mainland system. The protestors learned implicitly that dialogue with the government was fruitless, as it was not receptive to any views besides their own (meaning those of Beijing), and only street actions at an unprecedented level eventually made the authorities listen and withdraw the extradition bill. An insight with plenty of historical precedents from revolutionary uprisings.

From a western perspective, what the protestors sought appears mundane, even obvious; just a fair society, both in terms of its political and legal system, where human rights are upheld, and which are underpinned by the rule of law to which everyone is held accountable and not compromised by economic or politically-vested interests. Demands that Carrie Lam found impossible to recognize as they threatened 'national security', in their interpretation being defined as Beijing's right to meddle in pretty much everything. The high degree of autonomy that Hong Kong was promised in the handover agreement is something that the CCP mentions less and less. It is rarely seen in official communiques. Instead, they have introduced a new requirement for Hong Kong politicians, administrators, judges, and other judicial personnel to 'love the motherland', a euphemism which means unquestioned obedience to the leadership of the CCP, a prerequisite that might later even require a membership in the party to be eligible for public office.

As the volatile year of 2019 came to an end, it was becoming increasingly clear that Carrie Lam and Beijing had no intention of making any concessions to, at least some, of the protestor's demands, and might even be willing to discuss the prospects of universal suffrage. This as giving in to poplar pressure might make the party look weak, and they fear it could set a dangerous precedent that could be applied also on the mainland.[41] China has even rejected the most insignificant of the protestors demands, an independent inquiry into police brutality. It appears not to seek to heal the rift, but instead to impose its will by superimposing the Hong Kong judicial system with overarching national security laws, in effect harmonizing the two systems at their most disparate point, namely human rights.

What many feared materialized at China's top legislative body, the National People's Congress annual meeting, held in May 2020, where a draft national security act was presented for debate and voted on. The outcome of the vote was a forgone conclusion in this one-party setting. While the details of the proposal had not been fully spelled out in the draft, the gist of the law is to "prevent, frustrate, and punish any secessionist or subversive activity, the organizing of terrorist acts, and other acts that seriously threaten national security, as well as activities of foreign and external interference in Hong Kong," with the enforcement being administered by mainland Chinese security agencies operating inside Hong Kong. This proposal is by legal experts considered a breach of Article 23 of the Basic Law, which stipulates that Hong Kong is to pass security laws "on its own." The broad brushed terms in which national security laws in China are formulated mean that almost anyone is at risk of being targeted, such as the law against subversion that includes anyone *spreading rumors or slanders or any other means* with a view to subvert state power.

Effectively, any critique against the CCP falls under such stipulations, and by being handled by mainland security agencies, notoriously corrupt and where forced confessions, extending to torture, are an integral part of the investigation routine, it forebodes a society operating on fear, coercing and silencing all opportunities to free speech and debate. Not only would it apply to political matters, but would also influence commercial affairs where accusations, regardless of merits, of subversion always would be tilted in favor of the party with the closest link to the secret police. It would also subject foreigners residing, temporarily or permanent, in Hong Kong to it. As the proposed legislation takes aim at preventing alleged foreign interference, they would always be at a disadvantage. In short, it would eliminate much of what Hong Kong leaders has claimed to be its business advantages; an impartial and incorruptible rule of law, free from political influences and the safeguarding of human liberties. The city would be subjected to the same hardship conditions and repressions that few deny exist on the mainland.[42]

Many Hong Kongers now have the feeling of being under siege, with the opportunity to protest against unfair policies and free speech will be gone for the foreseeable future.[43] This crisis was solely the CCP's making, a clumsy heavy-handed approach, showing contempt for an agreement it had promised to live by, and having no interest nor understanding of the will of the population. This conflict has left Hong Kong facing its most severe existential crisis, with social fabrics in disarray, and much left in limbo. The incompetence of Carrie Lam's regime remains, spilling over to her sponsors in Beijing. It has also led many of the young generation to consider whether there is a future at all in Hong Kong, an exodus the city can little afford given its hastily ageing population and need for a well-educated creative workforce.

What is worse for the CCP is that the events in Hong Kong have not gone unnoticed by many mainlanders, so far keeping silent or covertly supporting the protesters, rather than the pro-Beijing government. And it provides the explanation to the often almost hysterical responses from Beijing and the local government, the fear that the demands for democratic reform will also reach the mainland, incited by the relatively nouveau riche middle class thirsting for more freedom. Hong Kong might prove to be the spark that starts a prairie fire about to spread to the mainland also with unforeseen consequences. The CCP was caught by complete surprise by the scale and depth of the resentment that resonated amongst so many segments of society and found themselves united against oppression. Why were they not able to foresee it despite ample resources for monitoring public sentiment? How one measures the pent-up anger that risks spilling over in revolt and threatens society itself is something that the next chapter will deliberate on.

Chapter 6

How to Understand China's Psychosocial Conditions

"The people will save their government, if the government itself will allow them."

— Abraham Lincoln, 16th President of the United States, (1809-1865)

Following the usual protocol for faltering dictatorships, when the economy no longer can deliver as expected and disappointments can be noted among the *hoi polloi*, Xi Jinping has increased his hold on power, trying to instill fear in the citizens with a brutal clamp down on any signs of what the CCP considers to be transgressions. And if the rate of success is measured through the number of dissident incidents, where in the end few citizens dare speak up against injustices and the denial of human rights, the CCP's strategy has so far been successful. But quite literally under the surface, the increased repression is building resentment and anger, seeking triggers, however mundane, to implode.

The CCP is now in dire need of soul searching, it was a communist party that utterly failed communism as self-inflicted poverty and despair forced it to reject its core ideological foundations. As a rescue, it took upon itself to become a nationalist party. It claims a monopoly on defining 'Chineseness', including what political views it should entail.

That idea, of course, is an impression that is rejected by Chinese in Taiwan, Hong Kong, the diaspora, and increasingly on the mainland itself. The definition of being Chinese is not to exempt oneself from human rights, that is merely a preposterous CCP claim to cling on to power. In fact, throughout its century long history, the party has spent most of its time rejecting what historically has been seen as Chinese values rooted in Confucian philosophy. As an integral part of the Cultural Revolution, it made a point of destroying as many ancient artefacts and antiques as possible. Contradictions, often glossed over or censored from being debated, have become part of the CCP's modus operandi as its core ethos has been absolute power and enriching its leadership.

But the mechanics of absolute power has rested on the erroneous assumption that the Chinese are standardized, truly small cogs in an enormous machinery, easily replaceable if not deemed satisfactory. Such philosophy has had horrendous consequences when applied as part of communism, or more recently nationalism. However, this perspective might have reached the end of the road, as further economic upgrade rests on promoting individual uniqueness, something highlighted by the superstars of Silicon Valley and others. Fostering individualism and self-fulfillment in all its forms is the very definition of the 'American Dream', usually reduced to the term 'freedom' that has allowed for the knowledge based economy to flourish. However, the concept of the 'Chinese Dream', as launched by the CCP, explicitly excludes such concepts. Instead, a central planned engineering-like approach still very much dominates its thinking. It simply shows a surprisingly poor understanding of the human psychology, a discipline that has never been a priority or area of focus in Chinese academia, often brushed off as Western humbug set to undermine Chinese societal harmony. An arrogant and deliberate omission which might prove costly as the requirements of creativity and innovation have highlighted.

When studying the collapse of the U.S.S.R., one of the lessons learned on the demise of the regime was that it allowed itself to fall apart from within, as infighting became rife when the economy and society decayed. In the Chinese view, this infighting was provoked to spring into action by some CIA-led destabilizing operation. The CCP has at times subscribed to the theory that it was Ronald Reagan's arms race that eventually caused the collapse of the U.S.S.R.; while not formally driving them into bankruptcy, or even a recession, it helped to stagnate the economy, and that was all it took for the U.S.S.R. to start to crumble. It is in this context that President Trump's trade war is interpreted. It is not about ensuring a level playing field in trade, but there are ulterior motives behind it, namely to contain China and eventually overthrow the CCP. Drawing on the historical perspective of the U.S.S.R., such an event can unfold in only a few years. To the CCP, the insight is that its survival depends on maintaining high morals and acting stoically against Western influences and its allure of civil liberties.

Forecasting China's Collapse According to Academic Theory

The academic studies on regime collapses suggest that an array of factors must occur to commence a societal demise. These typically include an economic slowdown, or at least stagnation, a highly corrupt bureaucracy and government, widening socio-economic inequalities, vested interests, whether they be of an ethnic, regional, or religious nature, and, implicitly at least, a breakdown of nationalist sentiments, with a preference for foreign cultures.[44]

There are sinologists who argue that China exhibits all of these factors to varying degrees, but simply because they are in place does not mean that regime collapse is imminent. Previous predictions have so far proven erroneous in timing at least. History highlights that the likely inciters of uprisings are the well-educated offspring of the middle class that have been lucky enough to be shielded from previous generations economic hardships, but feel bereft of basic human rights, and have started to identify themselves with their international peers with which they share cultural preferences and lifestyle choices rather than the elderly domestic generation. This young generation appears anxious and insecure, given the noted imbalances between their relative economic gains and lack of political rights, typically manifested in mental un-health and a postponement of family formation.[45]

There are further elements that segregate this younger middle class generation from the rest of the population. They typically live in richer coastal cities, like Shanghai, they tend to work in the private sector rather than in the governmental bureaucracy, and only a small percentage of them have joined the CCP. In total, this socio-economic class now make up about 5 percent of the population, estimated to be above 72 million in a 2016 survey, but only about 3 million of them are CCP members, and how many of these are members out of career reasons rather than political conviction is anyone's guess. They have become a domestic economic powerhouse, estimated to own more than half of China's intellectual property, and earn more than twice the national average, paying more than a third of all taxes.[46]

However, this group feels unsatisfied with their lack of political influence, and are to some extent voting with their feet, leading to capital outflow, and in some cases emigration, many seeking Hong Kong as a point of refuge given its up until recently greater degree of freedom. It has been with great worry that the CCP is observing the events now unfolding in Hong Kong, where this young, well-educated generation has radicalized, a fair share of them born and educated on the mainland, and taken to the streets protesting against political oppression and demanding democratic reforms and a restoration of human rights. The greatest fear of Beijing is that these sentiments will, in a contagious manner, spill over to the mainland and lead to demands for increased political rights.

Even prior to the outbreak of the Corona virus and its negative impact on the economy, many experts pointed to a brewing financial crisis in China. It being caused by a combination of economic misfortunes, namely its high and growing debt levels versus the relatively low GDP per capita. It has been exacerbated by the ongoing trade war, which everyone understood was not going to be completely resolved, the lack of innovative capacity, and an adverse demographic situation, with an aging and shrinking population. All factors that leave China at the risk of getting caught in the middle income trap, without being able to economically establish a welfare state, and having to abandon many of its ambitious global aspirations, such as the Belt-and-Road nowadays rarely mentioned in party media.

Much of its income will also have to be dedicated to unproductive sectors; the armed forces, which are being upgraded in what appears to be an emerging arms race with the U.S. and its Asian allies, and the costs of taking care of the elderly, a non-productive and fragile age group that already stands at about 18 percent of the total population. In accumulation, a hefty financial burden that will not help to progress the economy but risks further indebting China. But despite all the hallmarks of financial calamities in the making, predicting the timing of an economic recession, extending to crisis, is notoriously hard, and many renowned economists have lost their glory and fame making predictions of coming collapses that failed to materialize at the prophesized time. The complexities of an economy, even a largely state-controlled one, with its many variables acting in concert in unpredictable ways, makes it close to impossible to forecast the timing and duration of its peaks and troughs.

A heavily indebted nation, especially if mainly relying on domestic borrowing, can always further indebt itself for decades before the feared Minsky Moment arrives. While such structural balance sheet factors need not reach the point of no return, the insight that they hold the propensity to do so can, and have historically, at times, caused societal distress and the downfall of regimes. Studies of collapsing empires and civilizations stretch back millennia, and plenty has been written about the fall of the Roman Empire, the French and Russian revolutions, and more recently the collapse of communism in Eastern Europe, the Arab Spring and the Color Revolution. These studies are a source of constant worry for dictatorships as they are void of the political electoral cycle and can therefore not get a sense of its citizen's changing political preferences. The fact that it has proved so hard to project the trigger points of these downfalls often lead authoritarian leaders to establish excessive vigilance and a control apparatus that through the burden they put on everyday life itself often result in violent public eruptions.

Most conflict theories and studies on civilization collapses note a distinct change in psychological sentiments, often between generations, that trigger a resentment towards reigning morals and values, and begins confronting them, subliminally at first with ensuing open confrontation at later stage. Thus, changing underlying psychological factors stand as the root cause to bring about revolutions, or similarly, as a response to increasing levels of misery or sense of injustice, and is sometimes referred to as the *frustration-aggression theory.*

One of the more famous hypotheses of this psychological perspective on conflict was that of the American sociologist James Davies (1918-2012) who proposed a *J-curve,* indicating that political violence had its roots in the aggregate feeling of relative deprivation due to expected economic improvements which 'suddenly' failed to materialize. Hence, the name J-curve, prolonged uptrends of economic and social improvements are succeeded by period of sharp reversal which graphically depicts the letter J. This reversal creates an expectation gap and a heightened level of frustration that carries the risk to evolve into a revolutionary mood and the launch of political violence amongst the masses. According to Davies, what decides political stability or instability is the nature of the collective mood, however the state of dissatisfaction is relative, in other words, there are no absolute material boundaries for when frustration can set in. If applying the J-curve to an economic growth trend, one should thus be able to pinpoint quite precisely in time when there is an increased risk of an eruption of revolutionary activity and political violence. Therefore, revolutions are likely to occur after a period of good economic times followed by a sudden decline of fortunes, which was not discounted for, irrespectively of absolute levels of wealth.[47]

The gist of these theories is that a continuous build-up of social or psychological discontent eventually must give forth unless the regime is able mentally to disarm these sentiments by injecting remedies of a psychological well-being nature. But the historical fact is that the typical default response is to address public vexation with increased political oppression, which further adds fuel to an already inflammable situation. It evolves as a two-step process; a change of sorts in the present stagnating situation differing from the past, and that this newly arisen situation presents an opportunity for a revolution to take place. So, whatever factor, whether economic, political, or social, that was previously insufficient to trigger political violence, now holds that capacity. However, this is not a deterministic assumption. If the reigning regime is astute enough to sense the change in psychological sentiments, they can prevent public uprisings from occurring through instituting reforms.

When psychological stagnation has set in a society, it is reflected in cultural manifestations, among others, as creative artistic endeavors are heavily confined into a few, or rather too few, acceptable areas. It is often striking to outside visitors how dull and lifeless the art scene has become, predictably following highly ritualized and stereotype patterns, lacking that dynamic vibrant feel. In Chinese society, like that of the former Soviet Union, cultural life has largely become sterile and stale, with any new artistic productions being strictly self-censored. From the perspective of the CCP, the requirements to censor art deemed morally and politically dangerous takes on a highly paternal approach, treating its citizens as hapless children who without oversight can be led astray.

In the party's view, it is assumed that there is something delicate in the Chinese psyche that easily can be swayed into misdeeds and therefore a constant vigilance is needed to keep these apparently irresistible urges at bay. The contemporary Chinese art scene is mostly theatrically and cinematically performing the old classics, and not seldom with a nationalist twist, producing only kitsch-like lifeless exhibits that promote acceptable political axioms, which by some domestic artists, like Ai Wei Wei, eventually came to evolve into acts of subversive affirmation as a way of protest. And filmmakers, authors, and artists are under increased scrutiny, with obvious self-censorship working non-stop to appease the party's cultural minders. It stands in stark contrast to, for instance, the dynamic South Korean cultural scene, mostly prominent through its wide variety of K-pop and soap operas that have become huge export successes in the region.

You Just Entered a Psychologically Repressive Environment

A psychologically repressive environment is defined through increasingly dogmatic beliefs that have come to dominate the public discourse, and to openly criticize or confront them comes with the risk of being ostracized, maybe sentenced to lengthy imprisonment, or even worse. As the restricted narrative increases, the taboo areas (what cannot be publicly discussed) expands correspondingly. To circumvent these, euphemisms are increasingly deployed. Slogans and the propaganda used to promote the reigning doctrine, over time, become ever simpler and, for an outsider, incomprehensible as the words used often defy their original meaning, producing nothing but banalities.

The public discourse devolves into what is, in effect, infantilism. With a psychologically repressive environment gaining foothold, a risk averse attitude comes to dominate the population, as the peril of being at odds with the regime is simply too high. Thus, parts of reality are being repressed in an 'Emperor's New Clothes'-type syndrome. In the end, as a coping mechanism, people start to give up, and passivity becomes the preferred way of life. As such, mental stagnation kicks in. Over time, there is a noted increase in the number of psychological ailments, and also an alarming increase in cases of alcohol and drug abuse.

Behavioral Changes – Neurosis

The repression of perceptions not allowed by an authoritarian regime is found in various acts of self-deception, which is a process of either denying or rationalizing away logical arguments that contradict a subscribed belief or values. Reality is purposely misinterpreted, in particular the perceptions of one's own relation to it. It is often done to convince oneself of a certain view of reality that has turned into an unquestionable truth. Part of this self-deception might occur unconsciously, so that any awareness of it is not obvious. These periods of self-deception can last for a long time and often carry with them severe consequences, as perceptions of reality tend to become skewed and misaligned. And by truncating reality and omitting parts of it, eventually irrational behavior enters, meaning that a lot of decision-making will operate on paradoxes.

For some, this can eventually become overwhelming and psychological disturbances can develop. Some of these psychological disturbances can evolve into self-destructive behavior, including a wide array of acts from mutilating oneself to various forms of substance abuse, eating disorders, and ultimately successful or unsuccessful suicide attempts. One can expose oneself to adverse lifestyles and thought patterns that will lead in the direction of abuse, exploitation, and pain, whether of a physical or psychological sort, and is referred to as low self-esteem or self-hate. As the repressive society considers evermore topics taboo, delusions serve as a fitting behavioral mechanism. This in order to uphold the pretext of normality in such a psychologically unbalanced environment, where they are allowed to form a highly-adapted interpretation of reality to ensure the adherence to dogmatic beliefs.

Delusion is a psychiatric term, albeit rarely used nowadays, highlighting the manifestations of erroneous ideas about reality, either about oneself or the external world, which by the objective bystander is considered not to be true. In essence, the delusional ideas can only be categorized as absurd. What characterizes delusions is that they are expressed with an unusual conviction to the point that any disagreeing evidence will rarely convince the affected of the conviction's falseness. They come to play a defining part in the life of the individual or collective, with humor and irony generally frowned upon, even met with aggression, in particular when the delusional ideas are being challenged.[48]

Many of the psychological conditions that manifest in repressive environment falls under the label *neurosis*, including anxiety, hysteria, distress, phobias, and obsessive disorders, often highlighted as anger, irritability, sadness, or depression, but also as compulsive acts and inappropriate behavior. As it covers so many symptoms, it has been hard to systematically track over time and between cultures. The upholding of a degree of normalcy in a psychological unsound society requires denying some instinctual needs, and therefore comes to incorporate neurosis as an integral part of society. But as it results in anxiety and distress, it is therefore not a desirable compromise between society's culture and human instincts. Hence, there are hypocritical aspects of societal life that stand as the root cause to neurosis. Neurosis, while a today rarely used labelling, belongs to a category of mental ailments that are described as cultural diseases which are defined according to the following criteria:

> Is being viewed as a disease exclusively occurring in a certain era and context and is being labelled and spread within a defined culture with its norms, narratives and threats;

> Most of its symptoms are of a diffuse character and cannot be biologically verified, and;

> It vanishes over time as it is no longer regarded as a disease by the medical expertise, or another cultural disease replaces it due to changing circumstances.[49]

Sometimes given the vague properties, the malaise is, at times, classified as general fatigue or a type of depression.

Radicalization Means Destruction and Renewal

In a psychologically detrimental setting, whether individually or collectively, radicalized acts often set in as a remedy to break the rut, seeking disruption and destruction rather than the previous assertive and passive lethargic attitudes. This radicalization is highly uncompromising and it emerges in its own set of black-and-white discourses with defined scapegoats and highly confrontational rhetoric. Radicalization goes hand-in-hand with mental unhealth, as both are symptoms of a mentally repressive society, typically by restricting the freedoms to express oneself, whilst the former is turned inwards, the latter is attacking the source of the problem, namely society and its gatekeepers. These destructive forces only awaken in certain fertile breeding grounds, namely a society or culture whose norms have evolved into something too rigid and too lifeless. It is an environment unwilling to bend to changing realities, this as certain values have been declared irreproachable and their interpretations have become strict and obstinate.

Even when it should be apparent to its endorsers and enforcers that the outcomes they produce go against any good judgment and any common sense, the emotional and financial capital that they have invested into these dogmas make it difficult to let go of them, and hence little is ever done. Obviously, the unyielding attitude to adhering to these norms as they have regressed to inflexible edicts of sorts is a more viable prospect in a political dictatorship. This as authoritarian leaders can impose their will through means of controlling the state apparatus and media with demands of self-censorship, rather than in a culturally and politically pluralistic society.

Hindsight analysis of the ideologies that come to dominate in stagnating periods appear often surprisingly trite, with their simpleton slogans often so watered down in content that they come to mean anything, or rather nothing. The shallow propaganda, which from the objective interpretation only points to a void, in effect highlighting a sterile society, might be one of the first signs of a faltering society. The dogmatic ideological tenets mindlessly parroted by their most ardent supporters become so dumbfounded and detached from reality that they are left staring into an abyss. In such a pathological environment, psychopaths easily climb the career ladder and come to dominate many senior echelons, further exacerbating the mental imbalance of society much as the theory of political ponerology suggests. The increased levels of infantilism and naivety that forms the political discourse is something that can be assessed and analyzed through the language deployed in publications, such as official bulletins, and the regime-controlled media. It is observed through more and more topics being painted in black-

and-white, turning many into fanatics, as well as growing numbers of taboos that come to blind out parts of reality.

What follows after an extended period of stagnation that has been allowed to linger on, without any serious attempts by the government to alleviate these dissatisfactions, causing psychologically detrimental effects, is radicalization. It is a process that unfolds over years, even decades. Anecdotal evidence points to changes in the shared perception of reality as the spark to the inception of what was previously regarded as an unlikely set of actions. Something must have prompted a change in the collective mindset that suddenly opens the mental door for the acceptance, or at least passive endorsement, of a profound break of existing norms and social codes, often including an escalating element of destructiveness and violence, typically following the aforementioned J-curve path. Thus, one need look at cases where the perception of the proverbial cup as half-full changes to half-empty, basically where confronting the existing order with destructive behavior becomes a conceivable path of recourse, often the trigger point might seem to be of a relatively trivial nature, such as the introduction of a new piece of legislation.

Such a sudden transition from abiding by the reigning norms to a pathological mood might, however, often appear puzzling. In essence, the destructive activities are, absurdly enough, remedies as they seek to address an impaired psychological situation by externalizing and articulating what has been repressed, allowing for it to emerge and being appropriately dealt with. There is paradoxically something psychologically healthy in the concerted efforts to provoke conflicts with a pent-up release of aggressions as these activities have been demonstrated to hold therapeutic qualities. And whilst such insights might be disturbing from a strictly moral consideration, it reflects the true psychological make-up of the human nature, so what is seen as good and bad can therefore not be viewed as fixed or absolute values, but they are relative and conditioned by how society performs in terms of providing their citizens mental comfort.

As the radicalization phase commences, the newly radicalized pro-actively seek confrontation and conflict rather than avoiding it, no longer sidestepping or even deliberately ignoring issues that previously would have been brushed aside and repressed. The radicalized come to act with no intent for compromise and operate on a black-and-white worldview where all blame is directed against a spelled out and well-defined enemy. The fanaticism tends to increase with the perceived hopelessness of the situation. In that sense, destruction rather than be-ing victorious is what fuels the behavior and can be characterized as the modus operandi of an uncompromising zealous religious sect, such as:

Aggression, any critique is vehemently dismissed;

Aversion towards outsiders;

Alienation, and;

Absolute truth.[50]

Radicalization aims to reject the governing political power by un-dermining its foundation, in which violence serves as one means to an end. It is often claimed that one not only radicalizes toward extreme ideas or ideals, but that it must be relativized against the status quo it is targeting. From the perspective of the ruling ideology, the idea to radi-calize will always be deemed as extreme and often also irrational.[51]

But while a society's collective psychological make-up is not that easy to objectively measure, there are some psychological factors that can be identified through proxy metrics, and give indications on the col-lective mental status, including:

Suicide rates

Levels of mental ill-health

Birth rates

Alcoholism/Drug Abuse

Life expectancy

However, with the exception of birth rates and life expectancy, these statistics come with quite significant measurement problems, and their interpretations are not always straight forward, as the phenomena they represent often are considered as taboos. Hence, it is not unusual for regimes with the power to influence their bureaucracies to sometimes prevent an embarrassing statistic from being reported or enforce changes to its definition so that to study the trend is no longer possible. Some go so far as to outright falsify statistics to reverse negative trends. There are however supranational organizations, most notably the World Health Organization (WHO), that standardize definitions and collect data from member states on an annual basis, which provides more reliable statistics that can be used for trend analysis. For example, a metric that measures mental ill-health carries a conspicuous stigma in many countries, and thus one must assume cases being under-reported, making cross-country comparisons difficult.

Metrics can also deviate within a country/culture over the decades as the definitions of what constitutes mental illnesses differ and generally have expanded considerably over time. Albeit, that in itself can arguably be a sign of a mentally stagnating society and therefore need not skew the statistical analysis. In some countries, such as in the former Soviet Union, certain mental illnesses, like sluggish schizophrenia, were part of the political psychiatry and dissidents could be punished by being locked up in psychiatric wards accused of being mentally ill because of their political views. But to declare certain political views as equivalent to mental illnesses is a sign of repressiveness in a society and would therefore also not distort the trend analysis. Mental ailments also tend to trend with the economic peaks and troughs, suicides notably increasing during economic recessions. Hence, one needs to distinguish cases where prolonged economic depressions lead to psychological ailments and cause a surge in suicides as a result of high unemployment numbers, personal bankruptcies, or other economic difficulties. So, adverse psychological developments can occur without a collective mental stagnation activating, as these increases tend to recede hastily as economic conditions improve and can therefore be differentiated. Thus, the increasing trends in deteriorating demographic metrics therefore need to transcend the economic cycle.

Hong Kong versus China – a Study of Psychosocial Conditions

Most existing conflict theories directly or implicitly point to changing psycho-social conditions as a trigger to political violence. What previously did not cause psychological ill-health or aggravation suddenly do. Either as pent-up and repressed negative feelings that have not been allowed an acceptable outlet from the point of view of the reigning norms, or events have escalated to the proverbial boiling point. It will require that individuals and collective alike take action to rectify a mentally unstable situation, often that comes to mean destroying an unhealthy status quo and the powers that sustain it. This deterioration proceeds along a trajectory that can be monitored and, through proxy metrics, measured with the aspiration to try to time episodes where the risk of political violence becomes rampant. Some of these metrics are relatively straightforward, however, as mentioned previously, given their contentious nature, at least in certain regions, it is far from certain that they objectively represent the conditions on the ground. Thus, they are marred with measurement problems which could be significant. Albeit their absolute values might underrepresent the true numbers, the direction of the trends over time is still likely to be correct, especially if all these metrics concur in terms of tendencies. For the mental stagnation phase, it would include:

Number of cases of mental illnesses

Number of alcoholism incidences

Number of narcotic incidences

As the final phase of radicalization begins, further metrics can be added:

Number of suicides

Birth rates

Life expectancy

All of the above metrics should highlight adverse trends over a multi-year time period.

Birth Rates

North Asian countries have long had birth rates far below the replacement rate of 2.1, being among the lowest in the world, with an aging and shrinking population as a consequence. China, however, differs as it is so far behind in terms of economic status, as its GDP per capita is still only 20-25 percent of its richer neighboring countries. It has not yet been financially able to develop a welfare society capable of fully catering to the needs of its elderly citizens. Also, China's one-child policy was considered by the CCP as an integral part in its economic development program. Only in 2015 were couples officially allowed to have a second child. But this has not increased birth rates, au contraire, and with further ongoing urbanization, as well as improvements in women's education levels, factors known to drastically reduce birth rates, near term projections are that China soon will have a mere 10 million children born per year, in essence a collapsing demographic situation with an economy that is not yet fully developed to handle such a dramatic reversal.

Often, economic factors are blamed for the unwillingness to start families, aggravated through relatively modest childcare subsidies and a general lack of family-oriented work arrangements. In Hong Kong, the exceptionally low birth rates are exacerbated by a basic lack of space, with cramped living conditions in which even the well-educated are having to live with their parents into their mid-30s, which in effect prevents those eager to start a family from having children. A recent survey conducted in Hong Kong showed that only 47 percent of fertile women were willing to have children, which highlights how the deteriorating psycho-social conditions have come to supersede natural instincts. The consequences have been dire. Hong Kong now only has around 60,000 child births per year out of a population of 7.4 million.[52]

Traditional views on family have also drastically changed on the mainland, and the CCP's attempts to encourage larger families to secure its demographic future are proving futile, as the younger generation appears to be revolt against these demands. Among the millennial Chinese generation, a 'single society' is emerging, much to the dissatisfaction of the government, manifesting not only in a lower number of child births, but also that the previously sacrosanct institution of marriage is hastily losing its popularity, with the number of registered marriages dropping from 13.5 million in 2013 to 10.1 million in 2018, according to the National Bureau of Statistics. And, the divorce rates are increasing from 1.3 million in 2003 to 4.4 million in 2017. Mainland researchers assign the reason for evaporating adherence to such norms and values to the idea that younger generations are seeking to express themselves as individuals and with non-traditional lifestyles able to enjoy freedoms outside of what traditionally has been expected of them. These aspirations for more freedom, ignoring previous practices, are of course an ill-boding omen for party officials, realizing that the quench for freedom is also likely to spill over to demanding more civic liberties and political rights.[53]

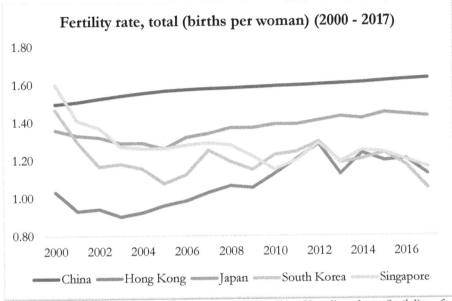

Figure 1) Fertility rate, total (births per woman) (2000 - 2017), China, Hong Kong, Japan, South Korea & Singapore. Source: The World Bank https://data.worldbank.org/indicator/sp.dyn.tfrt.in

Life expectancy

Life expectancies in North Asian countries are still on the rise with its citizens having among the highest longevity rates in the world. China is lagging behind its neighboring countries by six to seven years on average due to entering the industrialization phase about three decades later. But as later statistics and the birth rate highlight, the noted deteriorating psychological conditions can most clearly be observed among the young generation and can therefore, not yet, be observed in life expectancy numbers.

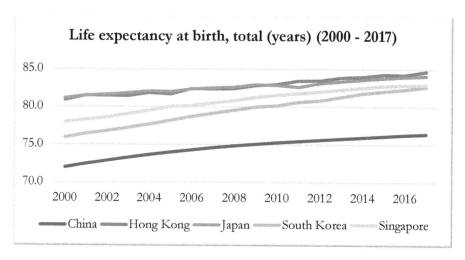

Figure 2) Life expectancy at birth (years) (2000 - 2017), China, Hong Kong, Japan, South Korea & Singapore. Source: The World Bank https://data.worldbank.org/indicator/sp.dyn.le00.in

Suicide rates

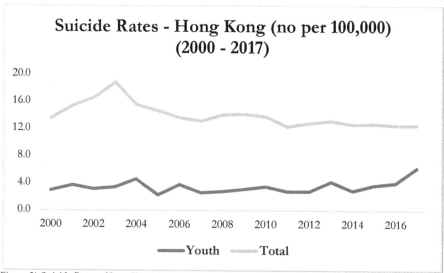

Figure 3) Suicide Rates - Hong Kong (no. per 100,000) (2000-2017) Youth versus Total. The number of suicides in 10-19 age group. Figures exclude injury undetermined whether accidentally or purposely inflicted. Source: https://www.socialindicators.org.hk/en/indicators/youth/30.4 & https://csrp.hku.hk/wp-content/uploads/2018/09/2018WSPD_slide.pdf

Suicide statistics need to be studied in context as they correlate, amongst others, with the age profile of the population, elderly citizens have typically significantly higher suicides rates than the younger generations, as well as, the economic throughs and peaks, as highlighted in figure 3) where the total suicide rate increased drastically during the 2003 economic crisis triggered by the SARS virus. After this economic crisis subsided, the total suicide rate fell notably in Hong Kong and has basically remained flat over the last decade. Other North Asian countries share the flat trend line over the same time period, with China seeing a slightly falling overall trend. This has been explained as due to lower number of rural women committing suicide, traditionally a high-risk suicide group in China, but as many have migrated to urban areas, away from family pressures, the suicide rates have dropped significantly for this segment, enough to move the overall trend downwards.

The data from China remains sketchy and must be interpreted cautiously. However, there is one significant trend that breaks previous correlations and that can be noted across the region, the surge in youth suicides, which shows similar increases as that of Hong Kong. Experts generally point to increased pressure in the educational system and contagion effects from social media as causal factors. As the intellectually demanding schools have been in place for generations, and peer pressure always existed, the explanations come across as perfunctory and lacking in depth. The trigger must lie elsewhere.[54]

Mental Ill-Health

Mental health problems, such as anxiety and depression, have been on the rise in Hong Kong over the last years. Estimates are now that as many as one in eight might be suffering from the aforementioned psychological ailments, which according to some experts might "probably be an under-representation, as stigma and shame prevents many people from reporting (problems with) mental health." Thus, at any count, a societal-wide problem with society-wide consequences and repercussions. Stigmas and under-reporting notwithstanding, the demand for psychiatric services has increased by 18 percent, from 187,000 cases in 2011 to over 220,000 cases in 2016. And the number of cases for child and adolescent psychiatric teams has increased by more than half in five years: from 18,900 in 2011 to 28,800 in 2016.

The local media have sporadically covered increases in mental unhealth with the acclaimed root causes seen as stressful work conditions, pressure for youngsters to intellectually perform in school, with excessive amounts of home works and tests, and the difficulties of entering the property ladder in what is the world's most expensive real estate market. The financial, educational, and work-related pressures are seen as taking its mental toll, as they have been allowed to linger on over an extended period of time with little done by politicians to alleviate the deteriorating situation. They have, on the contrary, been pouring petrol on the fire with constant promises of providing ease to the financial burdens, but as many of them are in the pockets of the tycoons, any promised changes have merely been of a cosmetic nature, if any at all. This has further worsened the psychological situation as few see much hope of a brighter future in an increasingly repressive politically self-serving system that seeks only to profit the wealthy elite at the expense of the masses and that takes its direct orders from Beijing.

Further estimates from two studies conducted in 2018 indicate that at least one in six Hong Kongers suffer from some mental disorder. The studies highlighted that a reported 60 percent experienced work-related stress and anxiety. It has become a city that is at the edge of a psychological cliff, with the political leadership being either in denial or completely neglecting the situation. And as with the suicide rates, the mental problems are notably higher among the younger generation, where one in three young Hong Kongers suffers from stress, anxiety, or depression, as the Hong Kong Playground Association survey shows.[55]

Similar trends of increasing mental ill-health, in particular among the youth, can also be noted in Japan, Singapore, and South Korea, but as the social perception and stigma is still prevalent, adequate resources and an openness to discuss the issues are overall lacking, which means that treatments are at best sporadic, and often non-existent, translating to the region having the highest suicide rates in the world.

For mainland China, as with its suicide rates, the data is patchy and conclusive conclusions are hard to establish. However, a national survey between 2013 and 2015 assessing the prevalence of mental disorders, including mood disorders, anxiety disorders, alcohol-use and drug-use disorders, schizophrenia, and other psychotic disorders, eating disorder, impulse-control disorder, and dementia, indicate that these overall are on the rise. Over 16 percent of the over 32,000 respondents, across regions in China's first nationwide study, showed signs of mental disorder, excluding dementia, with anxiety disorders being the most common, in particular affecting the young generation disproportionally hard. The researchers blamed the increase in depression and anxiety on the idea that "rapid social change is likely to bring about a general increase in psychological pressure and stress," however there is obviously no mention of the impact of increasing political oppression. Trends that tally with developments in the neighboring countries, but compared with major developed countries, the percentage of Chinese people who will suffer from mental illness at some point in their lives is still relatively low.[56]

Another study indicates that at least 30 million youths, from ages between 7 to 18, have experienced emotional or behavioral problems, including depression and self-harm. In 2012, it was estimated that about 173 million people lived with a mental disorder, around 13 percent of the population, and while the Chinese government has tried to expand its mental health facilities, it is still very far from providing sufficient mental care institutions and psychiatrists. And due to traditional values, many suffering from mental ill-health avoid seeking help, even if it can be made available, evidenced by the study that highlighted that over 90 percent of people suffering from mental disorder have never been treated.[57]

Alcoholism & Narcotics Addictions

In Hong Kong, the total number of registered drug abusers has seen a falling trend, from over 13,000 in 2007 to around 6,600 persons in 2018. This shrinking trend is also mirrored in the number of persons arrested for drug offences during the same period. However, a recent survey conducted on the young generation suggests that below the surface of registered drug abusers, which usually only represent the tip of the ice berg, the number of students claiming to have used drugs has gone up by 23 percent compared to the poll three years earlier.[58]

Alcohol consumption per capita has remained largely flat according to the latest statistics. Similar developments in terms of narcotics and alcohol consumption/abuse are noted in the rest of the North Asian region, with indications that drug abuse among the young is on the rise, however the metrics are inconclusive.

Is Heaven Withdrawing its Mandate?

According to Chinese superstition, the longevity of an empirical dynasty coincides with a mandate from heaven, and when the divine forces have decided that their time is up, it is usually marked by a series of unfortunate events that heralds its downfall. It was the task of wise sages through divination to interpret auspicious signs that pointed to a reverse in fortunes. It is, of course, fully possible that the wisest of the wise sages saw through the mumbo jumbo and used the label 'mandate from heaven' as a euphemism to describe imperial incompetence causing various failures, this to avoid directly critiquing them, a precarious undertaking then, as it is today, coming with the risk of losing one's head. But one need not to be an ancient Chinese sage to notice foreboding signs of an ominous nature for the current self-proclaimed 'emperor' Xi Jinping. Since the commencement of his reign, the bad fortunes seem never ending, as one recedes, a new one emerges, with the regime not doing much else than firefighting. Not everything can be classified as incompetence, they have had some bad luck, most recently the outbreak of the corona virus.

The economy was bound to slow down at some point, with an over 30-year-long economic expansion without any noted protracted recessions. But already prior to the corona pandemic, China's economic position appeared more vulnerable than previously thought, few economists actually believed the statistics being presented, with at least parts of the economy appearing to be no more than a *Potemkin façade*. It came across as dubious as to why they kept spending so much on infrastructure when there were already enough bridges leading to nowhere and building apartment blocks no one ever intended to live in. All this was being developed only for the reason of keeping the workforce busy, fueled by heavy borrowing by the state, corporations, and households alike, which have reached unprecedented levels of debt for their stage of economic development.

The boastful CCP propaganda communiques claiming China as a center of creative excellence actually have little to show in terms of actual products and services being uniquely Chinese innovations. The colossal Belt-and-Road project that was intended to change trade routes in China's favor is rarely talked about nowadays, and the aspiration to build a modern welfare state had to be scrapped more than a decade ago, as the insight was dawning that China simply cannot afford it. It now has an aging and dying population with only 14 million children being born last year, in all hardly features of an up and coming superpower.

The corona crisis has obviously made an already vulnerable situation worse, with some economists estimating, or rather guessing, that the unemployment rate now can be as high as 20 percent and is likely to keep rising. With fueling tensions with the rest of the world, the party now drastically seeks to reform the economy, seeking growth from domestic consumption rather than exports. Having factored in that increased hostilities between China and its major trading partners is likely to continue, a possible worldwide recession hampering international trades over the next few years, and Western firms moving manufacturing from the country, decoupling in both economic and political terms superficially appears to be a sound strategy.

If so then something will have to give as they are seeking to match a global market of 6 billion potential consumers outside China, with its domestic consumer base consisting of 1.4 billion, which is a shrinking, and with a large segment being above 60 when consumption typically drops. It might ultimately lead to China no longer having a trade surplus but result in receding exports and still having to import commodities and higher end goods which it has not yet been able to produce locally. Add to this, a savings rate is unusually high, which it must be as there is no adequate welfare protection, and the GDP per capita number (versus the OECD) is far too low for most Chinese households to ever go out on a spending spree. It also carries the risk that China comes to eliminate more and more of the market mechanism and returns to central planning to dominate economic decisions.[59]

But it is not only the economy that is troubling the Chinese leadership, but also its faltering relationship with pretty much the rest of the world. Rarely has a country's goodwill deteriorated with such speed as China under Xi Jinping's helm. It is remarkable that it has managed to alienate itself so completely. This is in great contrast to the Soviet Union that had a following among a raft of third world countries aspiring toward establishing a similar socialist system, and also included a small but very vocal group in mainly Western Europe that were staunch communists working hard on promoting their worldview. But China has nothing of that, why is it? The reason is likely twofold: they have, like under Mao Tse Tung, no enticing political vision to offer, many points to China now being nothing more than a kleptocracy, seeking to primarily enrich primarily its leaders preferably at the expense of the rest of the world, with much of its trade deals in Africa for instance being referred to as neo-colonialism. It also makes a point of dressing all its policies in ethno-nationalistic Chineseness where foreigners simply cannot apply, even if they would like to.

Hence, over the last few years there is a growing antipathy towards the CCP in the West, which President Trump cleverly managed to articulate and use to his advantage in the 2016 U.S. presidential campaign, and eventually resulted in a still ongoing trade war, where the E.U. has endorsed the U.S. position despite its generally negative view of the Trump administration. This as both the E.U. and the U.S. have been net losers vis-à-vis China in global trade, some due to sloppiness but there are widespread accusations of predatory trade practices, forced transfers of intellectual property which has been outright copied, extending to extensive industrial espionage. There is a feeling that China is not obeying to rules others have to, and this is costing a lot of employment.

Also, under Xi Jinping's leadership, the severe political oppression and withdrawal of the already very limited freedoms have not gone down well in the West, with accusations of genocide in Xinjiang, forced human organ harvesting of political prisoners, and the withdrawal of human rights in Hong Kong. All this reflects very poorly on the CCP, and it is rare to hear any international endorsement for its policies, other than the odd shady businessman whose fortunes rest with blessings from the party. It would be a career ending move for a politician to do so. And China's response to foreign criticism has not helped either. Many of China's diplomats in effect becoming its worst enemies, where they on various forums have delivered thinly veiled threats, often using hysterical language, and sometimes, such as the Chinese ambassador to Sweden, uttered direct death threats, to anyone raising criticisms, responses that only have furthered the negative view of the Chinese regime.

The (mis-)handling of the Corona virus outbreak has furthered the distrust of the CCP with accusation that it deliberately withheld information, and coerced the WHO to downplay the risks during the initial stage, allowing for the virus to spread outside China. Now with the world busy trying to contain the virus at great cost, both financially and in human lives, the day of reckoning has not yet arrived. However, once the most acute phase is over and the pandemic is beyond its peak, with the death tolls, bankruptcies, and unemployment gauged, a post-mortem will take place figuring out the *why*, the *how* and most importantly the *who*. This is an exercise likely to be auspiciously coinciding with the U.S. presidential election campaign, prompting the mourners of the dead, the unemployed, and the financially ruined to seek retribution, even vengeance.

Political survival in the West (and possibly other countries) will hinge on pointing fingers at the CCP, and international pressure on them will mount, all seeking financial compensation in one way or another, such as debt write-offs, tariff hikes, or even direct contributions. There are ample means to strong-arm China to financial submission from taxation of Chinese imports to outright expropriation of Chinese assets abroad recognized to be under CCP control (which are virtually all of them) and boycotts across all sectors; commerce, culture, diplomacy, and sports with the Beijing Winter Olympics of 2022 being a potential first target. The CCP might sense what is about to happen, but there is actually very little they can do about it beyond trying to fiercely contest the accusations. They have so little support abroad that in the end they might go for the default Chinese way of isolation, simply not having to deal with troublesome foreigners any longer, something which the Great Wall stands as a historical testament to.

From Socialism with Chinese Characteristics to Fascism with Chinese Characteristics?

Today, the CCP remains communist in name only, in practice they had to abandon their take of Marxism-Maoism decades ago as they defaulted on its practical implementation, in the end it brought only misery and death to millions of Chinese. Instead, they opted for a sort of state-controlled capitalism fused with aggressive jingoism, for a long time economically successful as long as it was endorsed by international goodwill but which has now come to prove highly detrimental for its international relationships, standing at an all-time low. So, where does the CCP place itself on the ideological chart?

The 70th anniversary of the founding of the People's Republic of China celebration held in Beijing in 2019 gave cues of a political movement defined by a personal cult and the endorsement of violence as a mean to achieve its ambitions. Maybe it was not deliberate, but much of the celebrations had noted similarities with the choreography displayed in Leni Riefenstahl's Triumph of the Will (*Triumph des Willens*) portraying the Nazi Party Congress in 1934. The film clips took aim at distinguishing between the leader up on the podium and the sea of people below saluting him, the leader commanding and the masses obeying with all signs of individual traits erased, one easily replaced by another. It depicts faces of joy of being part of this collective organism. To this came hours of military displays, in straight lines parading past the leader's podium, highlighting endless strength.

The impression is that of a mechanized, in minute detail rehearsed, performance. But as much as it was perfectly performed, it was also completely lifeless, with no signs of spontaneity and originality. The participants of this celebration, like the participants of the Nazi Party rallies at the time, probably did not realize that when a political movement's preferred means of manifestation is sterile artistic kitsch, even macabre in its expressionless mode, it has always foreboded a society soon to be immersed in mayhem and destruction. It appears that authoritarian ideologies by default gyrate towards such arrangements. Its *raison d'être* requires it, as by seeking to control so much of its population, they aspire to establish a society more similar to that of a machine rather than a living symbiosis, where everything must operate according to script with collective human displays giving a distinct lifeless feeling, morbid in character.

And the rhetoric at the 70th anniversary matched that of the Nazi Party Congress; we have been humiliated by sinister international forces but have now risen and our unprecedented strength and success was due to, and can only continue, through the genius of our leader, and anyone trying to confront our mother/fatherland again, better beware. Xi Jinping's speeches were heavily interspersed with fight talk, much more than any of his recent predecessors, and an eagerness to confront both internal and external enemies, something which has not been heard since the times of Mao Tse Tung. The history of the CCP was also heavily redacted, in effect omitting their first three decades in power, no mentioning of the disasters such as the Great Leap Forward and the Cultural Revolution, which cost the lives of millions of Chinese. Excluded also were former party leaders and high-ranking officials such as Hua Guofeng, Hu Yaobang, and Zhao Ziyang that have fallen from grace for various political reasons and are now considered non-entities.[60]

For anyone that watched this spectacle and has studied Xi Jinping's speeches, what has the CCP now become? Is it a sort of fascist movement, albeit perhaps with Chinese characteristics both in form and content? The American historian Robert O. Paxton, one of the leading re-searchers on fascism, outlined in his milestone work *The Anatomy of Fascism* the defining characteristics of a fascist movement:

> a sense of overwhelming crisis beyond the reach of any traditional solutions;

> the primacy of the group, toward which one has duties superior to every right, whether individual or universal, and the subordination of the individual to it;

> the belief that one's group is a victim, a sentiment that justifies any action, without legal or moral limits, against its enemies, both internal and external;

> dread of the group's decline under the corrosive effects of individualistic liberalism, class conflict, and alien influences;

> the need for closer integration of a purer community, by consent if possible, or by exclusionary violence if necessary;

> the need for authority by natural chiefs (always male), culminating in a national chieftain who alone is capable of incarnating the group's historical destiny;

> the superiority of the leader's instincts over abstract and universal reason;

> the beauty of violence and the efficacy of will, when they are devoted to the group's success, and;

> the right of the chosen people to dominate others without restraint from any kind of human or divine law, right being decided by the sole criterion of the group's prowess within a Darwinian struggle.[61]

Certainly, most of the above defining criteria seem to apply to the current CCP, but to what degree and where there are noted deviations must be matter of debate, as trying to pin down the tenets of an ideology against a template can never be an exact exercise. Few would dispute that China has become an increasingly intolerant society over the last few years. Their melodramatic glorification of strength and violence that are deployed oppress and ruthlessly crush perceived internal enemies, and continuously pointing to some vague foreign conspiracies, are all hallmarks of what is understood as fascism.

Xi Jinping has made a deliberate choice to put political control ahead of business, and it is a choice that is costing the Chinese economy dearly both internally and externally. Many senior CCP members themselves have vast business empires and are now suffering, so internal resistance, maybe more out of business rather than political reasons, is brewing. There are thus reasons for the Chinese leadership to worry, as few other countries have such a history of internal infighting and bickering among rival factions jockeying for power.

What's Next for the CCP?

The adverse directions of many psychosocial metrics are similar across North Asian countries, highlighting a deteriorating mental environment. This is especially true for the young generation, with suicides, mental unhealth, alcoholism, and narcotic addictions, all showing alarming increases. Added to this, comes an unwillingness to start families, with child births very far below the replacement rate, meaning that all these countries are now facing a bleak demographic future. These shrinking and aging populations come with dire consequences, also for the economy. In short, it is a gloomy picture of dying societies in more than one way.

But why have widespread protests, including political violence, erupted in Hong Kong and not in the other countries? Or is it that Hong Kong is a harbinger of expected social unrest also being an imminent scenario awaiting them as well? Or could it be that Hong Kong differs meaningfully from its neighboring countries, which means that its fate can possibly be spared them? In Hong Kong, the advent of the destructive psychological forces has advanced beyond self-inflicted harm and is now directed towards a government as incompetent as it is unwilling to rectify the mentally detrimental milieu generated through the existing extreme economic, political and social injustices that have been allowed to fester. The ongoing phase of full scale radicalization and rebellion of the previously mainstream population is increasingly externally aimed against this culprit (meaning Carrie Lam and her puppet regime) with demands of being replaced with a psychologically more affable societal setting and leadership.

So far representatives of the government have failed to realize that it is its own policies that are the underlying root causes of the increasing mental distress, including suicides, and which has led to the alienation of its own citizens. Complaints against these policies have either been ignored or ridiculed by pro-government politicians, which has only furthered the frustrations. The local political system has been so crafted that there is in effect little or no opportunity for ordinary citizens to influence their living conditions. They are caged by vested economic and political interests that are proving highly divisive to a healthy psychological equilibrium. Not many alternatives are left to them, beyond emigration, other than to succumb to self-harm, basically having given up on society, themselves, and the prospects of ever having a family, or to take to the streets to destroy that which is destroying them. And now with the CCP seeking to make all forms of complaints and protests illegal, they are, unbeknownst to them, fueling the proverbial time bomb that is bound to be their undoing. But the party also is a victim of these circumstances, by being so caged by its own limiting doctrines that stand to prevent devising constructive solutions.

In contrast, the democratic systems in Japan, Singapore, South Korea, and Taiwan, can, to a much larger extent, accommodate its citizens' mental distress, or at least prevent them from turning to open revolt with unforeseen consequences. These countries are also noting a rise in adverse psycho-social conditions, which to some extent are due to structural economic factors caused by an increasing degree of automation in work places, now also extending into the high-level service professions of the middle class, create an enormous stress about which few politicians can do anything. But unlike Hong Kong, and the even more dictatorial China, they are equipped with representative parliaments, with appropriate checks and balances, and their more free-wielding cultures allow for and promote individual choices and independence, which are relatively adequate and sufficient devices to disarm the risk of rebellion. They provide for dynamic adjustments aligning, to some extent, with altering public appeals, and can diffuse pent-up bouts of anger in a timely manner. Hence, psychologically agitated citizens are both allowed, even culturally encouraged, to vent any disappointments with politicians and their policies through the polls without any risk of being ostracized, or even imprisoned. There is thus less of a need to continuously suppress one's own frustrations. An open society also holds fewer taboos to prevent perceived contentious topics from being publicly discussed, something that in itself carries healing therapeutic properties. This openness relaxes the constant requirements of adhering to and maintaining self-censorship. The externalization and projection of mental imbalances towards scapegoats is reduced as politicians, through various means, can be held accountable, and simply be voted out if they are not performing.

These mechanisms are lacking in Hong Kong and almost completely devoid in China, which means that public grievances are either outlawed or swept under the rug, pretending that they do not exist. However, a systematic tracking of psycho-social metrics as a tool to a people-oriented governing approach is non-existent in both China and Hong Kong, as the sole emphasis has been on various measurements of the economy which for the government have come to signify the only valid gauge of a society's well-being. On the surface, the prospects have, up until recently, looked splendid, with a strong economic growth, and in the case of Hong Kong negligent unemployment and cash abundant state coffers. So, from the government's highly limited point of view, all has been looking well, and thus the timing and magnitude of the protests could not have been fathomable based on the overall economic performance. The government's complete lack of awareness of the psychological conditions on the ground meant that their responses, summed up as arrogance and neglect, were bound to be unsatisfactory, and in fact became highly counter-productive, as they have instead come to aggravate the situation significantly and further radicalize the population.

The governing style of Carrie Lam's regime operates on a strictly bureaucratic and bookkeeping approach, with little of the human touch, and neither the acumen nor ability to cater to its population's psychological needs. A confrontational clash was therefore inevitable, only awaiting its appropriate trigger, which was the introduction of the extradition bill. The protesters pointed to the government as the scapegoat for the mental pressure they are suffering, which is, from a psychological perspective, an apt accusation. Is it in this light that forecasts can be made as to whether social unrests Hong Kong-style, or worse, can be expected also in mainland China?

With the CCP being one of the world's most oppressive regimes, second only to North Korea, and that has worsened under Xi Jinping, the answer is highly affirmative. Its educated middle class, with often an international flair, is likely to lead these protests, triggered by the same immense psychological force operating below the surface and mirroring the sentiments of its contemporaries in Hong Kong, which is poorly, if at all, understood by the leadership. As the CCP cannot understand the monster from within the Chinese psyche that they,

through their totalitarian policies, have hatched, and is about to be unleashed, they are instead embarked on a constant futile search for foreign conspirators and some sort of secret leadership coordinating coming revolts. But as the spark to such a rebellion truly comes from within,
much as the leaderless protests in Hong Kong have highlighted, and
indeed being no less mysterious in nature for its hapless governmental
observers, the regime will not be able to find an adequate remedy to
peacefully neutralize the demonstrators. Instead, it has to resort to a violent clampdown, maybe eventually to something akin to the drastic
Tiananmen Square style massacres that has left an open scar on the Chinese soul. Simply trying to bribe its citizens with cash handouts or
providing the superficial bread and circus solutions will and cannot alleviate these mental imbalances. Their lack of success will further frustrate the government, and as long as these shortcomings remain, the
collective mental forces dictate that the destruction of the system must
continue. It has become a question of survival from a mental health perspective.

The default response from both the governments of Hong Kong
and China so far has been to increase the oppression with varying degrees of violent means. Another transformation of the CCP into a version 3.0, more geared towards people-centric policies appears not to be
in the cards. Rather the opposite, as the Chinese leadership is demanding more conformism and collectivism. So, the CCP views with angst
the protests in Hong Kong as a potential precursor to what is to come
on the mainland as the drivers and demographics of the protests are
shared across the border.

But as the genie is now out of the bottle, and mainland China is
evidently entering a weaker economic phase, there are now two paths
that lie ahead for the CCP which will decide whether it can secure its
future as the dominating political force. The first path would be to meet
the psychological needs of the general public. To do this, the leadership

of the CCP needs to reform itself yet again, this time allowing for increased political and psychological freedoms, in particular allowing for a greater leeway in terms of providing conduits for individual self-fulfillment and to introduce psychological mitigants to reduce an increasing level of mental angst. However, the current CCP leadership, now mostly in their 60s and above, have yet to show any signs of a more agile management style that allows for removing parts of the hierarchical structure throughout society, and introducing de-centralization and a democratization of the political process. Their mindset remains deeply entrenched in a non-democratic, authoritarian, and strictly hierarchical approach, where any initiatives not emanating from approved sources and channels are viewed with great suspicion. Also, their ambitions are limited as the CCP can only offer materialistic solutions, aspiring towards a worker's paradise of sorts, that seeks to be all-encompassing, controlling, and with forced solutions on every aspect of the life stages from crib to cradle.

Herein, lies a problem for any political leadership so firmly grounded in materialism as the CCP. They are not equipped to deal with existential matters, such as the prospect of an afterlife, concerns that most humans eventually struggle with. Thus, there is an inherent weakness when a political ideology tries to replace a religion. By default, it always fails to meet mankind's perpetual spiritual needs, which explains the relatively short lives of political programs versus the millennia longevity of religion. So, despite the increased crackdowns on religious activities in China, they still grow amongst a population that has been denied spiritual values for a couple of generations now, through the different nominations of Christianity, Buddhism, Islam, Taoism, or Falun Gong. They hold a trump card as they can provide answers, or at least suggestions, to questions on which the CCP remains silent, making the party feeling threatened by its shortcomings. This is increasing the repression of alternative lifestyles and views, as China, as all totalitarian regimes, will not tolerate anyone to be different and original, and with the need to ensure that no one deviates from a certain standard, must develop an enormous control apparatus. It is costing several percentages of GDP, leading to a noted loss of productivity and a hindrance of the facilitation of creative and innovative ventures, also including the cultural scene.

In any authoritarian system, paranoia spreads easily, as the consequences of being ousted from political power is often fatal, sometimes extending also to one's family. As a result, conspiracy theories are rife, and protecting one's back by doing as little as possible becomes a viable survival mechanism. In such a psychological atmosphere, embarking on any creative and original ventures can only be done, if at all, with the utmost care, especially if it risks challenging many senior CCP member's political and economic interests. For those equipped with creative talents, the default option will be to remain passive and not to confront the party line. Hardly an enticing choice for them, nor for China, as it now seeks to upgrade its economy where it no longer copies existing products and services but provides creative thought leadership. Thus, a change in the current leadership appears unlikely.

Currently, and by consensus of all sinologist expertise, a change in leadership, or its policy, appears unlikely. However, the sinologist as the previous Kremlinologists tend to operate through a far too narrow perspective with a too intense focus on details, and often the wrong ones at that, to understand the bigger picture of an authoritarian highly bureaucratic political party. At this point in time, only two forecasts can be made with any greater certainty, namely, the CCP's hundredth anniversary to be held in 2021 is going to be a day to remember but probably not for the reasons the centenary expects, and the resilient Chinese people, known to survive extended periods of duress, will also get through the next crisis.

About the Author

Niklas Hageback has an extensive background in digital transformations and risk management. He has held regional executive management and project oversight roles at leading banks, including Credit Suisse, Deutsche Bank & Goldman Sachs, in both Asia and Europe, where he was in charge of a number of complex regionwide digital transformation & risk management initiatives. More recently, he has done extensive work in Artificial Intelligence, notably machine learning, leading the development of automated human reasoning & computational creativity applications. He has written extensively in a wide array of areas covering AI, Agile, behavioral finance, creativity, digital leadership, digital warfare, economics, risk management and psychology in its many aspects.

References

Chapter 1

Barnett, Thomas P. M. 2008. *Deng Xiaoping*. Esquire no. 4.

Deng, Xiao Ping. 30 June 1984. *Building a Socialism with a specifically Chinese character*. People's Daily. Central Committee of the Communist Party of China. http://en.people.cn/dengxp/ vol3/text/c1220.html (Accessed 1 February 2020).

Fewsmith, Joseph. 2013. *The Logic and Limits of Political Reform in China*. Cambridge, United Kingdom: Cambridge University Press.

Nathan, Andrew J. January 2003. *China's Changing of the Guard: Authoritarian Resilience*. Journal of Democracy. Johns Hopkins University Press. Volume 14, Number 1.

Nathan, Andrew J. January 2013. *China at the Tipping Point? Foreseeing the Unforeseeable*. Journal of Democracy. Johns Hopkins University Press. Volume 24, Issue 1.

Shambaugh, D. L. 20th April 2005. *Rising Dragon and the American Eagle*. Yale Global. https://yaleglobal.yale.edu/special-reports/us-election-world?id=5601 (Accessed 1 February 2020).

Shirk, Susan L. 1993. *The Political Logic of Economic Reform in China*. California Series on Social Choice and Political Economy. Oakland, CA: University of California Press.

Xu, Cheng Gang. December 2011. *The Fundamental Institutions of China's Reforms and Development*. Journal of Economic Literature 49(4).

Chapter 2

Bai, Chong-En, Chang-Tai Hsieh, and Zheng, Michael Song. 2016. *The Long Shadow of a Fiscal Expansion*. No. w22801. National Bureau of Economic Research.

Cuestas, Juan Carlos, and Paulo José Regis. August 2017. On the Dynamics of Sovereign Debt in China: Sustainability and Structural Change Economic Modelling.

Dikötter, Frank. 1998. Imperfect Conceptions: Medical Knowledge, Birth Defects and Eugenics in China. Columbia University Press, 1st edition.

Dollar, David. 3 - 5 June, 2015. *Institutional Quality and Growth Traps*. Pacific Trade and Development Working Paper Series Paper No. YF37-07.

Greenhalgh, Susan. 2008. *Just One Child: Science and Policy in Deng's China*. University of California Press.

Hasketh, Therese, Lu, Li & Xing, Zhu Wei. Sep 2005. *The Effects of China's One-Child Family Policy after 25 Years*. New England Journal of Medicine, 353 (11).

Hilton, Isabel. 15 June 2018. *Will China's Demography be its Downfall?* UnHerd, Global Affairs. https://unherd.com/2018/06/will-chinas-demography-downfall/ (Accessed 1 February 2020).

Huang, Cary. 24 March 2015. *How Lee Kuan Yew crafted Singapore into a role model for China*. South China Morning Post. https://www.scmp.com/news/china/article/1746072/how-lee-kwan-yew-crafted-singapore-role-model-china (Accessed 1 February 2020).

International Monetary Fund. April 2019. *World Economic Outlook Database* https://www.imf.org/external/pubs/ft/weo/2019/01 (Accessed 1 February 2020).

Kim, Byung-Kook (ed) & Vogel, Ezra F (ed). 2011. *The Park Chung Hee Era: The Transformation of South Korea*. Harvard: Harvard University Press.

Kuo, Lily. 17 January 2020. China's birthrate falls to lowest level despite push for more babies. The Guardian.

Krauss, Ellis S., and Pekkanen, Robert J. 2010. The Rise and Fall of Japan's LDP: Political Party Organizations as Historical Institutions. New York: Cornell University Press.

Lee, Amanda. 17 July 2019. *China's total debt rises to over 300 per cent of GDP as Beijing loosens borrowing curbs to boost growth.* South China Morning Post. https://www.scmp.com/economy/china-economy/article/3018991/chinas-total-debt-rises-over-300-cent-gdp-beijing-loosens (Accessed 1 February 2020).

Otsubo, Shigeru T. 2007. *Post-war Development of the Japanese Economy.* GSID, Nagoya University.

Ramo, Joashua Cooper. May 2004. *The Beijing Consensus.* The Foreign Policy Centre. https://web.archive.org/web/20130824150344/http://fpc.org.uk/fsblob/244.pdf (Accessed 1 February 2020).

Shambaugh, David. Fall 2016. *Contemplating China's Future.* The Washington Quarterly. 39:3.

Uk, Heo & Roehrig, Terence. 2014. *South Korea's Rise: Economic Development, Power, and Foreign Relations.* Cambridge: Cambridge University Press.

Wilson, Kevin. 11 September 2017. China Will Collapse from Economic Wasting Disease Long Before We Are Caught in Thucydides' Trap Seeking Alpha.

Xu, Xiang. & Han, Alice Siqi. February 2018. *Will China Collapse: A Review, Assessment and Outlook.* Economics Working Paper 18104. Hoover Institute, Stanford University.

Yu, Yongding. 2007. "亚洲金融危机的经验教训与中国宏观经济管理." *International Economic Review* (Chinese) 2007, no. 5 - 6.

Chapter 3

Bailin, Sharon. 1987. *Critical and Creative Thinking* (Informal Logic 9 (1)).

Chen, Lulu Yilun. 27 September 2018. *China claims more patents than any country but most are worthless.* Bloomberg https://www.bloomberg.com/news/articles/2018-09-26/china-claims-more-patents-than-any-country-most-are-worthless (Accessed 1 February 2020).

Cropley, D. H., Kaufman, J. C., & Cropley, A. J. April 2008. *Malevolent creativity: A functional model of creativity in terrorism and crime* (Creativity Research Journal 20).

Finnie, Peter. 11 February 2019. *Why China's impressive patent rates don't tell the whole story.* New States Man Tech. https://tech.newstatesman.com/guest-opinion/china-patent-rates (Accessed 1 February 2020).

Gino, Francesca & Wiltermuth, Scott S. February 18, 2014. *Evil Genius? How Dishonesty Can Lead to Greater Creativity* (Psychological Science).

Guilford, J. P. 1950. *Creativity* (American Psychologist, 5(9)).

Guilford, J. P. Winter 1967. *Creativity: Yesterday, Today and Tomorrow* (Journal of Creative Behavior).

Langley, P & Jones, R. 1988. A computational model of scientific insight (In Sternberg, R. J., ed., The nature of creativity: Contemporary psychological perspectives. Cambridge University Press).

Li Keqiang. 5 March 2015. *"Full Text: Report on the Work of the Government"* delivered at the Third Session of the 12th National People's Congress, Xinhua. http://news.xinhuanet.com/ english/china/2015-03/16/c_134071473.htm. (Accessed 1 February 2020).

Nisbett, Richard E. 2004. The Geography of Thought: How Asians and Westerners Think Differently and Why. New York, NY: Free Press; Reprint edition.

Runco, M. A. 2010. *Divergent thinking, creativity, and ideation,* in J.C. Kaufman & R. J. Sternberg, eds., *The Cambridge Handbook of Creativity.* New York: Cambridge University Press.

Ryan, Liz. 8 March 2017. *The Real Reason Your Employees Can't Innovate.* Forbes. https://www.forbes.com/sites/lizryan/2017/03/08/the-real-reason-your-employees-cant-innovate/#2f8cbf365af5 (Accessed 1 February 2020).

Simonton, Dean Keith. 1999. Creativity as Blind Variation and Selective Retention: Is the Creative Process Darwinian? (Psychological Inquiry, Vol. 10, No. 4).

Sulloway, F. J. 1996. Born to rebel: Birth order, family dynamics, and creative lives. New York: Pantheon Books.

Zha, Peija, et al. 2006. The Impact of Culture and Individualism–Collectivism on the Creative Potential and Achievement of American and Chinese Adults. Creativity Research Journal, Volume 18, Issue 3.

Chapter 4

Cook, Sarah. 27 February 2019. *Social credit scoring: How China's Communist Party is incentivising repression.* Hong Kong Free Press. https://www.hongkongfp.com/2019/02/27/social-credit-scoring-chinas-communist-party-incentivising-repression/ (Accessed 1 February, 2020).

Fifield, Anna. 3 August 2019. *Paramount and paranoid: China's Xi and the Communist Party face a crisis of confidence.* Washington Post. https://www.washingtonpost.com/world/asia_pacific/paramount-and-paranoid-chinas-xi-faces-a-crisis-of-confidence/2019/08/02/39f77f2a-aa30-11e9-8733-48c87235f396_story.html?noredirect=on (Accessed 1 February, 2020).

Łobaczewski, Andrzej. 2006. Political Ponerology: A Science on the Nature of Evil Adjusted for Political Purposes. Grande Prairie: Red Pill Press.

Repnikova, Maria. 27 November, 2018. *China's 'responsive' authoritarianism.* The Washington Post. https://www.washingtonpost.com/news/theworldpost/wp/2018/11/27/china-authoritarian/ (Accessed 1 February, 2020).

The Independent Tribunal into Forced Organ Harvesting from Prisoners of Conscience in China. 2019. *Final Judgement Report.* https://chinatribunal.com/final-judgement-report/ (Accessed 1 February 2020).

Chapter 5

Buddle, Cliff. Can we trust that Beijing's security law will target Hong Kong's violent minority only?

South China Morning Post. 25 May, 2020. https://www.scmp.com/comment/opinion/article/3085831/can-we-trust-beijings-security-law-will-target-hong-kongs-violent (Accessed 1 June 2020).

Campbell, Matthew. August 15, 2019. *Hong Kong's Massive Protests Raise Ominous Questions About 2047*. Bloomberg News. https://www.bloomberg.com/news/articles/2019-08-15/hong-kong-s-massive-protests-raise-ominous-questions-about-2047?srnd=premium-asia (Accessed 1 June 2020).

Gan, Nectar & Chow, Chung-yan. August, 16 2019. *Blindsided: why does Beijing keep getting Hong Kong wrong?* SCMP. https://www.scmp.com/news/china/politics/article/3022970/blindsided-why-does-beijing-keep-getting-hong-kong-wrong (Accessed 1 June 2020).

Lam, Jeffie. *Hong Kong Bar Association questions Beijing's legal power to enact national security law, identifies 'problematic' features*. South China Morning Post. 25 May, 2020. https://www.scmp.com/news/hong-kong/politics/article/3085991/hong-kong-bar-association-questions-beijings-legal-power (Accessed 1 June 2020).

Lo, Kinling. August, 21 2019. *The trouble with trying to turn Hong Kong's young people into 'patriotic youth'*. SCMP. https://www.scmp.com/news/china/politics/article/3023606/trouble-trying-turn-hong-kongs-young-people-patriotic-youth (Accessed 1 June 2020).

Marlow, Iain. August 5, 2019. *China's Xi Has Few Good Options to End the Chaos in Hong Kong*. Bloomberg News. https://www.bloomberg.com/news/articles/2019-08-05/china-s-xi-has-few-good-options-to-end-the-chaos-in-hong-kong (Accessed 1 June 2020).

Marlow, Iain. & Schmidt, Blake. August 7, 2019. *China Rejects One Demand That Could Help Ease Hong Kong Protests*. Bloomberg News. https://www.bloomberg.com/news/articles/2019-08-07/china-rejects-one-demand-that-could-help-ease-hong-kong-protests (Accessed 1 June 2020).

Mosher, Steven. W. July 6, 2019. *Hong Kong protests have sparked a new level of Chinese paranoia.* New York Post. https://ny-post.com/2019/07/06/hong-kong-protests-have-sparked-a-new-level-of-chinese-paranoia/ (Accessed 1 June 2020).

Chapter 6

Boeree, George C. 2002. *A Bio-Social Theory of Neurosis.* http://webspace.ship.edu/ cgboer/genpsyneurosis.html (accessed 1 June 2020).

Carothers, Thomas. 2002. *The End of the Transition Paradigm.* Journal of Democracy, no. 1.

Cheung, Elizabeth. 16 August, 2018. *Here's why Hong Kong's low fertility rate poses a threat to its very future.* SCMP https://www.scmp.com/news/hong-kong/community/article/2159874/heres-why-hong-kongs-low-fertility-rate-poses-threat-its (Accessed 1 June 2020).

Chu, Marian. 19 April 2018. *Stigmatizing mental illness leads to high suicide rate.* Korea Biomedical Review. http://www.koreabiomed.com/news/articleView.html?idxno=3043 (Accessed 1 June 2020).

Davies, James C. Feb 1962. "Toward a Theory of Revolution," *American Sociological Review*, Vol. 27, No. 1.

Ellström, Lars. Fascism med kinesiska kännetecken – om firandet av Folkrepubliken Kinas 60- och 70-årsjubiléer Nya Argus 5-6, 2020.

Griffiths, James & Watasuki, Yoko. 6 November 2018. *Japan's youth suicide rate highest in 30 years.* CNN. https://edition.cnn.com/2018/11/05/health/japan-youth-suicide-intl/index.html (Accessed 1 June 2020).

Huang, Y., et al. March 2019. *Prevalence of mental disorders in China: a cross-sectional epidemiological study.* Lancet Psychiatry. 6(3). p. 211 - 224. https://www.thelancet.com/journals/lanpsy/article/PIIS2215-0366(18)30511-X/fulltext (Accessed 1 June 2020).

Huntington, Samuel P. Summer, 1984. *Will More Countries Become Democratic?* Political Science Quarterly. Volume 99, No.

Hwee, Min, Ang. 5 August, 2019. *MOE, MSF 'very concerned' about spike in youth suicides; experts say more support and awareness necessary.* Channel News Asia. https://www.channelnewsasia.com/news/singapore/moe-msf-very-concerned-about-spike-in-youth-suicides-experts-say-11775260 (Accessed 1 June 2020).

Johannisson, Karin. 2008. *Om begreppet kultursjukdom.* Läkartidningen nr. 44. volym 105.

Johnston, Mark. 1995. Self-Deception and the Nature of Mind. Philosophy of Psychology (Debates on Psychological Explanation). Cambridge, United Kingdom: Blackwell Publishing.

Li, Cheng. September 2012. The End of the CCP's Resilient Authoritarianism? A Tripartite Assessment of Shifting Power in China. The China Quarterly, 211.

Linz, Juan Jose. 2000. *Totalitarian and Authoritarian Regimes.* Lynne Rienner Publishers. UK ed.

Liu, Marian. 29 April, 2018. *The secret burden of mental illness in Hong Kong.* CNN. https://edition.cnn.com/2018/04/29/health/mental-health-suicide-hong-kong-asia/index.html (Accessed 1 June 2020).

McLaughlin, Brian P., Oksenberg Rorty, Amélie. 1988. *Perspectives on Self-Deception (Topics in Philosophy).* Berkeley and Los Angeles, California: University of California Press.

Ng, Desmond. 12 May, 2018. *Under pressure at home and in school, youths battle depression.* Channel News Asia, CNA Insider. https://www.channelnewsasia.com/news/cnainsider/under-pressure-at-home-and-in-school-youths-battle-depression-10226122 (Accessed 1 June 2020).

Ng, Kang-chung. 29 October 2018. *Mental health in Hong Kong at worst level in seven years, with almost half scoring 'below passing mark', annual survey says.* SCMP. https://www.scmp.com/news/hong-kong/health-environment/article/2170743/mental-health-hong-kong-worst-level-seven-years (Accessed 1 June 2020).

Nishi, D., Ishikawa, H. & Kawakami, N. August 2019. *Prevalence of mental disorders and mental health service use in Japan.* Psychiatry Clinical Neuroscience. 73(8). https://www.ncbi.nlm.nih.gov/pubmed/31141260 (Accessed 1 June 2020).

Nylund, Karl-Erik. 2004. *Att leka med elden: Sekternas värld.* Sverige: Selling & Partner, 2., omarb. uppl.

Paxton, Robert O. *The Anatomy of Fascism* (New York: Alfred A. Knopf, 2004).

Pei, Minxin. 2016. *China's Crony Capitalism: The Dynamics of Regime Decay.* Cambridge: Harvard University Press.

Phillips, MR., Zhang, J., Shi, Q. et al. 2009. Prevalence, treatment, and associated disability of mental disorders in four provinces in China during 2001–05: an epidemiological survey. Lancet. 373. https://www.thelancet.com/journals/lancet/article/PIIS0140-6736(11)60893-3/fulltext (Accessed 1 June 2020).

Research Office, Legislative Council Secretariat. 2018. *Drug abuse in Hong Kong Statistical highlights.* ISSH28/18-19. https://www.legco.gov.hk/research-publications/english/1819issh28-drug-abuse-in-hong-kong-20190531-e.pdf (Accessed 1 June 2020).

Sha, Feng, et al. 2018. *Suicide rates in China, 2004 - 2014:comparing data from two sample-based mortality surveillance systems.* BMC Public Health. 18:239 https://doi.org/10.1186/s12889-018-5161-y (Accessed 1 June 2020).

Shambaugh, David L. 2008. *China's Communist Party: Atrophy and Adaptation.* University of California Press.

Shambaugh, David L. March 6, 2015. *The Coming Chinese Crackup.* Wall Street Journal.

Sum, Lok-kei. 6 June 2018. *One in three young Hongkongers suffers from stress, anxiety or depression, Hong Kong Playground Association survey shows.* SCMP. https://www.scmp.com/news/hong-kong/health-environment/article/2149403/one-three-young-hongkongers-suffers-stress-anxiety (Accessed 1 June 2020).

Wang, Xiaoyu. 24 May 2018. *Mental health issues rise among children*. China Daily. http://www.china-daily.com.cn/a/201805/24/WS5b0604b0a3103f6866eea3d8.html (Accessed 1 June 2020).

Wilner, Alex S. and Dubouloz, Claire-Jehanne. 2010. "Homegrown terrorism and transformative learning: an interdisciplinary approach to understanding radicalization". *Global Change, Peace, and Security*, 22:1.

Wong, Tsui-kai. 27 March 2019. *Teen drug use in Hong Kong is 'on the rise', according to survey.* SCMP, Young Post. https://yp.scmp.com/news/hong-kong/article/112442/teen-drug-use-hong-kong-%E2%80%98-rise%E2%80%99-according-survey (Accessed 1 June 2020).

Xu, Xiang. & Han, Alice Siqi. February 2018. *Will China Collapse: A Review, Assessment and Outlook*. Economics Working Paper 18104. Hoover Institute, Stanford University.

Yan, Alice. 10 August, 2019. *I don't' know why China's millennials are saying no to marriage.* SCMP https://www.scmp.com/news/china/society/article/3021964/i-dont-why-chinas-millennials-are-saying-no-marriage (Accessed 1 June 2020).

Yonhap. 26 April 2018. *Suicide No. 1 cause of death for S. Korean teens, youths.* The Korea Herald. http://www.koreaherald.com/view.php?ud=20180426000581 (Accessed 1 June 2020).

Zhang, Jie, et al. October 2014. *The Change in Suicide Rates between 2002 and 2011 in China*. Suicide and Life-Threatening Behavior. Volume 44, Issue 5. https://onlinelibrary.wiley.com/doi/abs/10.1111/sltb.12090 (Accessed 1 June 2020).

Notes

[1]Shambaugh, D. L. *Rising Dragon and the American Eagle*. Yale Global. 20 April 2005. https://yaleglobal.yale.edu/special-reports/us-election-world?id=5601 (Accessed 1 February 2020).

[2]Shirk, Susan L. *The Political Logic of Economic Reform in China California*. Series on Social Choice and Political Economy. Oakland, CA: University of California Press, 1993. Fewsmith, Joseph. *The Logic and Limits of Political Reform in China*. Cambridge, United Kingdom: Cambridge University Press. 2013.

[3]Xu, Cheng Gang. *The Fundamental Institutions of China's Reforms and Development*. Journal of Economic Literature 49(4). December 2011. pp. 1076-1151. Nathan, Andrew J. *China's Changing of the Guard: Authoritarian Resilience*. Journal of Democracy. Johns Hopkins University Press. Volume 14, Number 1, January 2003. pp. 6-17.

[4]Xu, Cheng Gang. *The Fundamental Institutions of China's Reforms and Development*. Journal of Economic Literature 49(4). December 2011. pp. 1076-1151.

[5]Barnett, Thomas. *P. M. Deng Xiaoping*. Esquire no. 4. 2008. p. 146.

[6]Deng, Xiao Ping. "Building a Socialism with a specifically Chinese character" in *People's Daily. Central Committee of the Communist Party of China*. 30 June 1984. http://en.people.cn/dengxp/vol3/text/c1220.html (Accessed 1 February 2020).

[7]Nathan, Andrew J. "China at the Tipping Point? Foreseeing the Unforeseeable," in *Journal of Democracy*. Johns Hopkins University Press. Volume 24, Issue 1, January 2013. pp. 20-25.

[8]Xu, Xiang. & Han, Alice Siqi. *Will China Collapse: A Review, Assessment and Outlook*, Economics Working Paper 18104. (Hoover Institute, Stanford University. February 2018).

[9]Yu, Yongding. "亚洲金融危机的经验教训与中国宏观经济管理." *International Economic Review* (Chinese) 2007, no. 5-6. 2007. pp. 5-8.

[10]Uk, Heo & Roehrig, Terence. *South Korea's Rise: Economic Development, Power, and Foreign Relations* (Cambridge: Cambridge University Press, 2014) p. 1 ctd. Otsubo, Shigeru T. *Post-war Development of the Japanese Economy* (GSID, Nagoya University, 2007) 12 ctd.

[11]Kim, Byung-Kook (ed) & Vogel, Ezra F (ed). *The Park Chung Hee Era: The Transformation of South Korea* (Harvard: Harvard University Press, 2011) pp. 629-651. Krauss, Ellis S., and Pekkanen, Robert J. *The Rise and Fall of Japan's LDP: Political Party Organizations as Historical Institutions* (New York: Cornell University Press; 2010) 115 ctd.

[12]Huang, Cary. *How Lee Kuan Yew crafted Singapore into a role model for China.* South China Morning Post. 24 March 2015. https://www.scmp.com/news/china/article/1746072/how-lee-kwan-yew-crafted-singapore-role-model-china (Accessed 1 February 2020).

[13]Greenhalgh, Susan. *Just One Child: Science and Policy in Deng's China* (University of California Press, 2008), chapter 1.

[14]Hasketh, Therese, Lu, Li & Xing, Zhu Wei. *The effects of China's One-Child Family Policy after 25 Years.* New England Journal of Medicine (Sep 2005) 353 (11), pp. 1171-1176. Dikötter, Frank. *Imperfect Conceptions: Medical Knowledge, Birth Defects and Eugenics in China* (Columbia University Press; 1st edition, 1998), chapter 4.

[15]Hasketh, Therese, Lu, Li & Xing, Zhu Wei. *The effects of China's One-Child Family Policy after 25 Years.* New England Journal of Medicine (Sep 2005) 353 (11), pp. 1171-1176. Kuo, Lily. *China's birthrate falls to lowest level despite push for more babies* The Guardian. 17 January 2020. Hilton, Isabel. *Will China's demography be its downfall?* UnHerd, Global Affairs. 15 June 2018. https://unherd.com/2018/06/will-chinas-demography-downfall/ (Accessed 1 February 2020).

[16]Hasketh, Therese, Lu, Li & Xing, Zhu Wei. *The Effects of China's One-Child Family Policy after 25 Years.* New England Journal of Medicine (Sep 2005) 353 (11). pp. 1171-1176. Hilton, Isabel. *Will China's demography be its downfall?* UnHerd, Global Affairs. 15 June 2018. https://unherd.com/2018/06/will-chinas-demography-downfall/ (Accessed 1 February 2020).

[17]International Monetary Fund. *World Economic Outlook Database* April 2019. https://www.imf.org/external/pubs/ft/weo/2019/01 (Accessed 1 February 2020).

[18]Lee, Amanda. *China's total debt rises to over 300 per cent of GDP as Beijing loosens borrowing curbs to boost growth.* South China Morning Post. 17 July 2019. https://www.scmp.com/ economy/china-economy/article/3018991/chinas-total-debt-rises-over-300-cent-gdp-beijing-loosens (Accessed 1 February 2020).

[19]Bai, Chong-En, Chang-Tai Hsieh, and Zheng, Michael Song. *The long shadow of a fiscal expansion.* No. w22801. National Bureau of Economic Research, 2016. Xu, Xiang & Han, Alice Siqi. *Will China Collapse: A Review, Assessment and Outlook.* Economics Working Paper 18104. (Hoover Institute, Stanford University. February 2018).

[20]Cuestas, Juan Carlos, and Paulo José Regis. *On the Dynamics of Sovereign Debt in China: Sustainability and Structural Change Economic Modelling,* August 2017. Wilson, Kevin. *China Will Collapse from Economic Wasting Disease Long Before We Are Caught in Thucydides' Trap.* Seeking Alpha, 11 September 2017.

[21]Dollar, David. *Institutional Quality and Growth Traps,* Pacific Trade and Development Working Paper Series Paper No. YF37-07. 3-5 June, 2015. Shambaugh, David. *Contemplating China's Future.* The Washington Quarterly. 39:3. Fall 2016. pp. 121-130.

[22]Ramo, Joshua Cooper. *The Beijing Consensus.* The Foreign Policy Centre. May 2004. https://web.archive.org/web/20130824150344/http://fpc.org.uk/ fsblob/ 244.pdf (Accessed 1 February 2020). Shambaugh, David. *Contemplating China's Future.* The Washington Quarterly. 39:3. Fall 2016. pp. 121-130.

[23]Nisbett, Richard E. *The Geography of Thought: How Asians and Westerners Think Differently and Why.* New York, NY: Free Press; Reprint edition. 2004.

[24]Cropley, D. H., Kaufman, J. C., & Cropley, A. J. *Malevolent creativity: A functional model of creativity in terrorism and crime* (Creativity Research Journal 20, April 2008) pp. 105-115. Sulloway, F. J. *Born to Rebel: Birth Order, Family Dynamics, and Creative Lives* (New York: Pantheon Books, 1996). Gino, Francesca & Wiltermuth, Scott S. *Evil Genius? How Dishonesty Can Lead to Greater Creativity* (Psychological Science, February 18, 2014).

[25]Guilford, J. P. *Creativity: Yesterday, Today and Tomorrow* (Journal of Creative Behavior, Winter 1967). Runco, M. A. *Divergent thinking, creativity, and ideation* (In J. C. Kaufman & R. J. Sternberg (Eds.), *The Cambridge handbook of creativity,* New York: Cambridge University Press, 2010) pp. 413-446. Simonton, Dean Keith. *Creativity as Blind Variation and Selective Retention: Is the Creative Process Darwinian?* (*Psychological Inquiry,* Vol. 10, No. 4, 1999) pp. 309-328.

[26]Bailin, Sharon. *Critical and Creative Thinking* (Informal Logic, 9 (1) 1987). Guilford, J. P. *Creativity* (American Psychologist, 5(9), 1950) pp. 444-454. Langley, P & Jones, R. *A computational model of scientific insight* (In Sternberg, R. J., ed., *The nature of creativity: Contemporary psychological perspectives.* Cambridge University Press, 1988) pp. 177-201.

[27]Ryan, Liz. *The Real Reason Your Employees Can't Innovate.* Forbes, 8 March 2017. https://www.forbes.com/sites/lizryan/2017/03/08/the-real-reason-your-employees-cant-innovate/#2f8cbf365af5 (Accessed 1 February 2020).

28Zha, Peija, et al. *The Impact of Culture and Individualism–Collectivism on the Creative Potential and Achievement of American and Chinese Adults* (Creativity Research Journal, Volume 18, 2006, Issue 3.), pp. 355-366.

29Chen, Lulu Yilun. *China claims more patents than any country but most are worthless.* Bloomberg. 27 September 2018. https://www.bloomberg.com/news/articles/2018-09-26/china-claims-more-patents-than-any-country-most-are-worthless (Accessed 1 February 2020). Finnie, Peter. *Why China's impressive patent rates don't tell the whole story.* New States Man Tech. 11 February 2019. https://tech.newstatesman.com/guest-opinion/china-patent-rates (Accessed 1 February 2020).

30Ibid.

31Li Keqiang. "*Full Text: Report on the Work of the Government*" delivered at the Third Session of the 12th National People's Congress, Xinhua. 5 March 2015. http://news.xinhuanet.com/english/china/2015-03/16/c_134071473.htm. (Accessed 1 February 2020).

32Łobaczewski, Andrzej. *Political Ponerology: A Science on the Nature of Evil Adjusted for Political Purposes* (Grande Prairie: Red Pill Press, 2006).

33Fifield, Anna. *Paramount and paranoid: China's Xi and the Communist Party face a crisis of confidence.* Washington Post. 3 August 2019. https://www.washingtonpost.com/ world/asia_pacific/paramount-and-paranoid-chinas-xi-faces-a-crisis-of-confidence/2019/08/02/39f77f2a-aa30-11e9-8733-48c87235f396_story.html?noredirect=on (Accessed 1 February 2020).

34Ibid.

35Cook, Sarah. *Social credit Scoring: How China's Communist Party is incentivising repression,* Hong Kong Free Press. 27 February 2019. https://www.hong kongfp.com/2019/02/27/social-credit-scoring-chinas-communist-party-incentivising-repression/ (Accessed 1 February 2020).

[36]Repnikova, Maria. *China's 'responsive' authoritarianism,* in The Washington Post. 27 November, 2018. https://www.washingtonpost.com/news/the-worldpost/wp/ 2018/11/27/china-authoritarian/ (Accessed 1 February 2020).

[37]The Independent Tribunal into Forced Organ Harvesting from Prisoners of Conscience in China. *Final Judgement Report* 2019. https://chinatribunal.com/final-judgement-report/ (Accessed 1 February 2020).

[38]Gan, Nectar & Chow, Chung-yan. *Blindsided: why does Beijing keep getting Hong Kong wrong?* SCMP. August, 16 2019. https://www.scmp.com/news/china/politics/article/3022970/blindsided-why-does-beijing-keep-getting-hong-kong-wrong (Accessed 1 February 2020).

[39]Lo, Kinling. *The trouble with trying to turn Hong Kong's young people into 'patriotic youth'* SCMP. August, 21 2019. https://www.scmp.com/news/china/politics/article/3023606/trouble-trying-turn-hong-kongs-young-people-patriotic-youth (Accessed 1 February 2020).

[40]Campbell, Matthew. *Hong Kong's Massive Protests Raise Ominous Questions About 2047.* Bloomberg News. August 15, 2019. https://www.bloomberg.com/news/articles/2019-08-15/hong-kong-s-massive-protests-raise-ominous-questions-about-2047?srnd=premium-asia_(Accessed 1 February 2020).

[41]Marlow, Iain. & Schmidt, Blake. *China Rejects One Demand That Could Help Ease Hong Kong Protests.* Bloomberg News. August 7, 2019. https://www.bloomberg.com/news/articles/2019-08-07/china-rejects-one-demand-that-could-help-ease-hong-kong-protests (Accessed 1 February 2020).

[42]Buddle, Cliff. *Can we trust that Beijing's security law will target Hong Kong's violent minority only?* South China Morning Post. 25 May, 2020. https://www.scmp.com/comment/opinion/article/3085831/can-we-trust-bei-jings-security-law-will-target-hong-kongs-violent (Accessed 25 May 2020). Lam, Jeffie. *Hong Kong Bar Association questions Beijing's legal power to enact national security law, identifies 'problematic' features.* South China Morning Post. 25 May 2020. https://www.scmp.com/news/hong-kong/politics/article/3085991/hong-kong-bar-association-questions-beijings-legal-power (Accessed 25 May 2020).

[43]Marlow, Iain. *China's Xi Has Few Good Options to End the Chaos in Hong Kong.* Bloomberg News. August 5, 2019. https://www.bloomberg.com/news/ articles/2019-08-05/china-s-xi-has-few-good-options-to-end-the-chaos-in-hong-kong (Accessed 1 February 2020).

[44]Huntington, Samuel P. *Will More Countries Become Democratic?* Political Science. Quarterly. Volume 99, No. 2. Summer, 1984. pp. 193-218. Linz, Juan Jose. *Totalitarian and Authoritarian Regimes* Lynne Rienner Publishers. UK ed. 2000. Carothers, Thomas. *The End of the Transition Paradigm,* Journal of Democracy, no. 1. 2002. pp. 5-21.

[45]Shambaugh, David L. *China's Communist Party: Atrophy and Adaptation.* University of California Press, 2008. Shambaugh, David L. *The Coming Chinese Crackup.* Wall Street Journal, March 6, 2015. Li, Cheng. *The End of the CCP's Resilient Authoritarianism? A Tripartite Assessment of Shifting Power in China.* The China Quarterly 211. September 2012. Pei, Minxin. *China's Crony Capitalism: The Dynamics of Regime.* Cambridge: Harvard University Press, 2016.

[46]Xu, Xiang. & Han, Alice Siqi. *Will China Collapse: A Review, Assessment and Outlook.* Economics Working Paper 18104. (Hoover Institute, Stanford University. February 2018).

[47]Davies, James C. *"Toward a Theory of Revolution,"* American Sociological Review, Vol. 27, No. 1 (Feb 1962), pp. 5-19.

[48]McLaughlin, Brian P., Oksenberg Rorty, Amélie. *Perspectives on Self-Deception (Topics in Philosophy)* (Berkeley and Los Angeles, California: University of California Press, 1988). Johnston, Mark. *Self-Deception and the Nature of Mind. Philosophy of Psychology (Debates on Psychological Explanation)* (Cambridge, United Kingdom: Blackwell Publishing, 1995) pp. 63-91.

[49]Boeree, George. C. *A Bio-Social Theory of Neurosis 2002.* http://webspace. ship.edu/ cgboer/genpsyneurosis.html (accessed 1 February 2020). Johannisson, Karin. *Om begreppet kultursjukdom* (Läkartidningen nr. 44. 2008 volym. 105) pp. 3129-3132.

[50]Nylund, Karl-Erik. *Att leka med elden: Sekternas värld* (Sverige: Selling & Partner, 2., omarb. uppl., 2004).

[51]Wilner, Alex S. and Dubouloz, Claire-Jehanne. "*Homegrown terrorism and transformative learning: an interdisciplinary approach to understanding radicalization.*" Global Change, Peace, and Security 22:1 (2010), p. 38.

[52]Cheung, Elizabeth. *Here's why Hong Kong's low fertility rate poses a threat to its very future.* SCMP. 16 August, 2018. https://www.scmp.com/news/hong-kong/community/ article/2159874/heres-why-hong-kongs-low-fertility-rate-poses-threat-its (Accessed 1 February 2020).

[53]Yan, Alice. *I don't' know why China's millennials are saying no to marriage.* SCMP. 10 August, 2019. https://www.scmp.com/news/china/society/ article/3021964/i-dont-why-chinas-millennials-are-saying-no-marriage (Accessed 1 February 2020).

[54]Zhang, Jie, et al. *The Change in Suicide Rates between 2002 and 2011 in China.* Suicide and Life-Threatening Behavior. Volume 44, Issue 5. October 2014. pp. 560-568. https://onlinelibrary.wiley.com/doi/abs/10.1111/sltb.12090 (Accessed 1 February 2020). Hwee, Min, Ang. *MOE, MSF 'very concerned' about* spike *in youth suicides; experts say more support and awareness necessary.* Channel News Asia. 5 August, 2019. https://www.channelnewsasia.com/news/ singapore/moe-msf-very-concerned-about-spike-in-youth-suicides-experts-say-11775260 (Accessed 1 February 2020). Griffiths, James & Watasuki, Yoko. *Japan's youth suicide rate highest in 30 years* CNN. 6 November 2018. https://edition.cnn.com/2018/11/05/health/japan-youth-suicide-intl/index.html (Accessed 1 February 2020). Yonhap. *Suicide No. 1 cause of death for S. Korean teens, youths.* The Korea Herald. 26 April 2018. http://www.koreaherald.com/ view.php?ud=20180426000581 (Accessed 1 February 2020). Sha, Feng, et al. *Suicide rates in China, 2004–2014: comparing data from two sample-based mortality surveillance systems.* BMC Public Health. 2018. 18:239 https://doi.org/10.1186/s12889-018-5161-y (Accessed 1 February 2020).

[55]Ng, Kang-chung. *Mental health in Hong Kong at worst level in seven years, with almost half scoring 'below passing mark', annual survey says.* SCMP. 29 October 2018. https://www.scmp.com/news/hong-kong/health-environment/ article/2170743/mental-health-hong-kong-worst-level-seven-years (Accessed 1 February 2020). Liu, Marian. *The secret burden of mental illness in Hong Kong.* CNN. 29 April, 2018. https://edition.cnn.com/2018/04/29/health/mental-health-suicide-hong-kong-asia/index.html (Accessed 1 February 2020). Sum, Lok-kei. *One in three young Hongkongers suffers from stress, anxiety or depression, Hong Kong Playground Association survey shows.* SCMP. 6 June 2018. https://www.scmp.com/news/hong-kong/health-environment/article/ 2149403/one-three-young-hongkongers-suffers-stress-anxiety (Accessed 1 February 2020).

[56]Ng, Desmond. *Under pressure at home and in school, youths battle depression.* Channel News Asia, CNA Insider. 12 May 2018. https://www.channelnewsasia.com/ news/cnainsider/under-pressure-at-home-and-in-school-youths-battle-depression-10226122 (Accessed 1 February 2020). Chu, Marian. *Stigmatizing mental illness leads to high suicide rate.* Korea Biomedical Review. 19 April 2018. http://www.koreabiomed.com/ news/art-cleView.html?idxno=3043 (Accessed 1 February 2020). Nishi, D., Ishikawa, H. & Kawakami, N. *Prevalence of mental disorders and mental health service use in Japan.* Psychiatry Clinical Neuroscience. August 2019. 73(8). pp. 458-465. https://www.ncbi.nlm.nih.gov/pubmed/31141260 (Accessed 1 February 2020). Huang, Y., et al. *Prevalence of mental disorders in China: a cross-sectional epidemiological study.* Lancet Psychiatry. March 2019. 6(3). pp. 211-224. https://www.thelancet.com/journals/lanpsy/article/PIIS2215-0366(18)30511-X/fulltext (Accessed 1 February 2020).

[57]Wang, Xiaoyu. *Mental health issues rise among children.* China Daily. 24 May 2018. http://www.chinadaily.com.cn/a/201805/24/WS5b0604b0a3103f6866 eea 3d8.html (Accessed 1 February 2020). Phillips, MR., Zhang, J., Shi, Q. et al. *Prevalence, treatment, and associated disability of mental disorders in four provinces in China during 2001–05: an epidemiological survey.* Lancet. 2009. 373, pp. 2041-2053. https://www.thelancet.com/journals/ lancet/ article/PIIS0140-6736(11)60893-3/fulltext (Accessed 1 February 2020).

[58]Research Office, Legislative Council Secretariat. *Drug abuse in Hong Kong.* Statistical highlights, 2018. ISSH28/18-19 https://www.legco.gov.hk/ research-publications/english/1819issh28-drug-abuse-in-hong-kong-20190531-e.pdf (Accessed 1 February 2020). Wong, Tsui-kai. *Teen drug use in Hong Kong is 'on the rise', according to survey.* SCMP, Young Post. 27 March 2019.
https://yp.scmp.com/news/hong-kong/article/112442/teen-drug-use-hong-kong-%E2%80%98-rise%E2%80%99-according-survey (Accessed 1 February 2020).

[59]Zhou, Cissy. *Coronavirus has hit China's migrant workers harder than Sars and the financial crisis, but worst yet to come.* South China Morning Post. 25 May 2020.
https://www.scmp.com/economy/china-economy/article/3085904/corona-virus-has-hit-chinas-migrant-workers-harder-sars-and (Accessed 25 May 2020).
Tang, Frank. *China's economic strategy shift shows Xi Jinping is preparing for 'worst case scenario', analysts say.* South China Morning Post. 25 May 2020.
https://www.scmp.com/economy/china-economy/article/3085969/chinas-economic-strategy-shift-shows-xi-jinping-preparing (Accessed 25 May 2020)

[60]Ellström, Lars. *Fascism med kinesiska kännetecken – om firandet av Folkrepubliken Kinas 60- och 70-årsjubiléer Nya Argus,* 5-6, 2020.

[61]Paxton, Robert O. *The Anatomy of Fascism* (New York: Alfred A. Knopf, 2004) p. 219 ctd.

HISTRIA BOOKS

GAUDIUM

GAUDIUM PUBLISHING
BOOKS TO CHALLENGE AND ENLIGHTEN

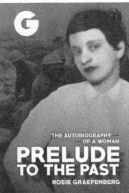

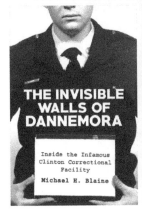

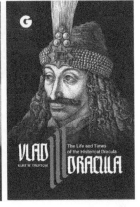

FOR THESE AND OTHER GREAT BOOKS VISIT
HISTRIABOOKS.COM